Steam in the Welsh Landscape

(Including Monmouthshire)

MICHAEL WELCH

Capital Transport

ISBN 978-1-85414-382-2

Published by
Capital Transport Publishing Ltd
www.capitaltransport.com

Printed by Parksons Graphics

Front Cover: Harlech castle provides an impressive background as BR Standard Class 4MT No.76040 departs with a down train which, judging by its quite long formation, could be the Pwllheli portion of the 'Cambrian Coast Express'. This picture dates from September 1966. The author, who was visiting this area at the period this picture was taken, remembers seeing this locomotive on the 'Cambrian' so, perhaps, it was a regular engine at the time.
John Spencer Gilks

Title Page: The Holyhead portion of an express from London, probably the 10.35am from Euston, with Stanier 'Royal Scot' Class 7P 4-6-0 No.46150 *The Life Guardsman* in charge, rushes across Bodorgan viaduct on a sunny day in May 1962. The carriage immediately behind the locomotive is a restaurant miniature buffet coach (classified RMB) which has a small counter for the service of light refreshments.
John Spencer Gilks

Back cover: Thunder at Commins Coch. Situated about halfway up the long ascent from Machynlleth to the summit at Talerddig, the fabulous scenery at Commins Coch made it a favourite vantage point for photography. Locomotives hauling heavy trains would always be working to their maximum and often produced magnificent smoke effects but on this occasion both engines are clearly being expertly fired: there is hardly a trace of smoke to be seen. *Colin Hogg*

Author's note: Many place names have been changed during the 120 year period covered by the captions in the book, and in order to avoid confusion, generally the spelling used by the railway company that originally promoted the route referred to is used throughout.

Introduction

On the morning of 4th March 1967 the overnight mail train from York (4.10am from Shrewsbury) rolled into Aberystwyth station behind BR Standard Class 4MT 4-6-0 No.75033. After the locomotive had been uncoupled from the train, turned on the turntable and serviced, a group of photographers descended on the engine with rags and paraffin and commenced the task of giving the locomotive a thorough clean, because this was the final day of standard gauge steam at Aberystwyth and No.75033's next working was the very last London-bound 'Cambrian Coast Express' – history was about to be made and the photographers did not want a dirty engine spoiling their pictures. Whilst standard gauge steam traction could still be found running along the North Wales coast main line, and in South Wales where the sound of National Coal Board locomotives still echoed across the valleys, from the 4th March, when the last steam trains ran between Shrewsbury and Aberystwyth, large tracts of Wales were henceforth operated solely by diesel traction (on those lines that survived) and steam had been totally banished, a transformation that had been achieved in less than ten years.

Without a doubt Wales had some of the most attractive railway routes in Great Britain and perhaps the best known of those that survived the Beeching cutbacks of the 1960s is the highly scenic Cambrian coast line from Dovey Junction to Pwllheli which links many small towns and resorts. Opened throughout in 1867, the line provides marvellous vistas as it hugs the coastline, but in the author's opinion the highlight of a trip along this splendid route is the crossing of Barmouth bridge which gives magnificent views up the unspoilt Mawddach estuary. When, in the early 1980s, the bridge was found to be unsafe the whole future of this line was in doubt but, mercifully, BR found the money to repair it and the route was saved. In steam days this line was operated by a variety of classes, including GWR 'Manor' 4-6-0s, 4300 Class 'Moguls' and 2251 Class 0-6-0s, but probably the most interesting locomotives to be observed were the archaic looking 'Dukedog' 4-4-0s that were really much more modern than their outside frames suggested.

Another lovely line that escaped closure is the Conway Valley line from Llandudno to Blaenau Festiniog. Unlike most other lines in Wales this branch was constructed under the aegis of the London & North Western Railway (LNWR), but construction of this route, which was originally planned to be narrow gauge, was beset by difficulties and the LNWR board probably rued the day when they decided to proceed with this costly adventure. The principal headache for the directors was the boring of a 3,861 yards-long tunnel just north of Blaenau Festiniog. Tenders grossly exceeded estimates so the LNWR instructed one of its own engineers to supervise the work which started in 1874 with the excavation of four shafts. After a momentous struggle this wonderfully scenic line finally opened in July 1879. A journey southwards from Llandudno is a fascinating experience offering stunning views of the mountains of Snowdonia but, in total contrast, the landscape at Blaenau Festiniog is almost completely dominated by the man-made mountains of slate that surround the town. Diesel units were introduced on this line at an early date but steam continued to work the goods trains until the mid-1960s.

Unlike the two aforementioned routes the 27½ miles-long branch from Whitland to Cardigan was a true backwater and, alas, one that has long since been erased from the railway map. Built in three distinct sections over a period of thirteen years, the first stretch from Whitland was constructed to serve slate quarries at Glogue and opened in 1873. Another section was opened for business two years later but it was not until 1886 that Cardigan was reached. This branch, which was cheaply built, followed the lie of the land and course of rivers, and was characterised by unbelievably sharp curves and stiff gradients, some as steep as 1 in 35. Built in the days when a horse and cart was the most common form of conveyance these drawbacks were of no consequence but the pathetically slow overall journey time of 1 hour 40 min., together with a very sparse service, could have done little to foster passenger traffic in the age of the motor car and the line was closed in September 1962 before 'Beeching' became a household name. A trip over this line, which connected a string of villages in a delightfully remote part of rural Wales, must have been a joy for aficionados especially as steam traction – usually GWR 4500 Class 2-6-2Ts or pannier tank engines – reigned supreme until the end.

But, perhaps, the most outstanding route in Wales was the Moat Lane Junction to Brecon line, a route of immense charm which was probably the most picturesque and best-loved line in the whole of the principality. Apart from short sections at the extremities, this line was built by the Mid Wales Railway and ran in splendid isolation all of the way from Moat Lane to Three Cocks Junction, a distance of 48¼ miles; the line from Hereford was joined at the latter location. Both stations served only a few cottages in their immediate vicinity and their main purpose was to act as interchange stations. The Mid Wales company had its headquarters at Llanidloes and the main focus of operations was also there because, in addition to a small engine shed that supplied the line's motive power, a few trains either started or terminated their journeys at Llanidloes which was one of the principal towns on the route. Some stretches of the line were exceptionally beautiful, particularly the remote section between Llanidloes and Rhayader where it followed the tumbling waters of the Afon Dulas and eventually crossed the watershed to join the tranquil river Wye, along which it ran for mile after mile, providing one of the most enjoyable and relaxing rail journeys imaginable. The line attained the height of 947 ft above sea level at Pantydwr, the highest station on the Cambrian Railways' system. Sadly, in the railway industry's harsh economic circumstances of the late 1950s the British Transport Commission did not consider it a duty to provide 'relaxation and enjoyment' on little-used country branch lines and the Moat Lane Junction to Three Cocks line was earmarked for closure along with all of the other routes that radiated from Brecon. This resulted in one of the most contentious and bitterly fought closure proposals in Great Britain and doubt was cast upon the losses quoted by BR: the Moat Lane line alone was said to be losing £290,000 per annum. Predictably, at a time when the motor car was 'king', and people in government seemed to believe that the rail network had no future, the Brecon closures were swiftly approved and the Moat Lane Junction line was closed at the end of 1962, and Wales lost one of its most charismatic lines.

Compilation of this album has been an immensely rewarding and enjoyable experience which has been heightened by the help and co-operation of numerous photographers, who not only had the foresight to take the pictures in the first place all those years ago but also willingly trusted me with their precious prints and transparencies so they could be enjoyed by a wider audience. In addition a number of enthusiasts have assisted with proof reading and suchlike and thanks are due to Chris Evans, Dave Fakes, John Langford, Graham Mallinson and Terry Phillips. The luggage labels were kindly provided by Les Dench. Thanks are also due to Mike Esau for providing pictures from the John Spencer Gilks and Colin Hogg collections and also Rodney Lissenden for the shots from the late R.C. Riley collection. Design and typesetting by Lucy Frontani.

Michael Welch
Burgess Hill
West Sussex
March 2014

Contents

BRITISH RAILWAYS BOARD (M) BR 4405

LLANFAIRPWLLGWYNGYLLGOGERYCHWYRNDROBWLLLLANTYSILIOGOGOGOCH

PLATFORM TICKET 3d.

AVAILABLE ONE HOUR ON DAY OF ISSUE ONLY
NOT VALID IN TRAINS. NOT TRANSFERABLE.

FOR CONDITIONS SEE OVER

B 78772

78772 B

| 1 | 2 | 3 | 4 | 5 | 6 | 7 | 8 | 9 | 10 | 11 | 12 |

Prior to the coming of the railways, mail between Great Britain and Ireland had to be carried overland by horse, and later coach, and movement was not helped by ferry crossings at Conway and the Menai Strait. Construction of two suspension bridges at those points eased the situation but the government was keen to improve the Irish mail service and routes to both Holyhead and Porth Dinllaen in Caernarvon Bay were surveyed. A government committee advised that George Stephenson's North Wales coastal route, from Chester to Holyhead, was feasible and on 4th July 1844 a bill allowing construction received the Royal Assent. The 'railway mania' year of 1845 saw some bizarre proposals, such as the London & Holyhead Railway's idea for a route from Banbury via Kidderminster, Shrewsbury and Capel Curig and on through the Llanberis Pass to join the proposed North Wales Railway; it was claimed that this would be much shorter than the Crewe and Chester route. Despite these crazy schemes, work commenced on the Chester & Holyhead Railway's line on 1st March 1845, and by August 1846 a total of 12,000 men were reported to be at work. A major task was the construction of bridges across both the Conway estuary and Menai Strait and, in order to provide the 100-feet clearance demanded by the Admiralty at the latter location, Robert Stephenson proposed the novel idea of tubular beams within which the trains would run. The Conway bridge was shorter and needed less clearance above the water so this was tackled first of all, the wrought iron tubes being assembled on the banks of the river and floated into position before being raised by hydraulic presses. The first of the Conway tubes was ready by April 1848 and shortly afterwards, on 1st May 1848, the 59¾ miles-long Chester to Bangor stretch was opened to passengers with four weekday trains being provided. The second tube was in position by January 1849. While work progressed on the Britannia bridge across the Menai Strait navvies were at work on the 20½ miles-long section from Llanfair PG to Holyhead and this opened on 1st August 1848 with through passengers between Chester and Holyhead being conveyed by coach across Telford's road bridge. Following completion of the Britannia bridge the entire line from Chester was opened, the 2.30pm Holyhead to London express being the first train through on 18th March 1850. In later years, and especially after holidays with pay became the norm for the masses, the string of resorts along the North Wales coast proved an irresistible attraction for generations of day trippers and holiday-makers. The train seen here, hauled by Stanier Class 5MT 4-6-0 No.45275, appears to be an additional summer extra train which was typical of many everyday workings during the early 1960s prior to the growth of continental holidays; these formed an endless procession on summer Saturdays. This picture was taken at Prestatyn on 18th August 1962. *Edwin Wilmshurst*

A view of the east end of Llandudno Junction station that is thought to date from the mid 1950s. This photograph seems to have been taken during a lull in traffic, note that all of the signals are in the 'on' position. The first station, opened in 1860, was 'vee' shaped and on a site slightly to the west with separate platforms for main line and Llandudno branch trains. The LNWR later decided to construct a brand new station to the east of the original premises and this was eventually finished in 1897. The Conway Valley branch connection had to be re-sited further to the east and a new carriage shed was built on the old trackbed. The tracks in the immediate foreground are through lines while those behind the station nameboard serve only short bay platforms normally used by branch services. There are more through tracks on the extreme right, almost concealed from view, and one of those serves a platform road. The signal box in the centre of the picture is Llandudno Junction No.1. The junction with the branch to Blaenau Festiniog is situated beyond the road overbridge. *Stuart Ackley collection*

Pictured from the battlements of Conway castle, an unidentified Stanier Class 5MT 4-6-0 bursts out of the western portal of the Conway tubular bridge; the locomotive is completely dwarfed by its majestic surroundings. The estuary of the river Conway forms a superb backdrop with distant hills beyond; the long buildings just visible across the water are Llandudno Junction engine and carriage sheds. The original station at Conway was closed from 14th February 1966 but a new station with much shorter platforms opened in 1987. *Stuart Ackley collection*

The North Wales coast main line certainly lives up to its name – the sea is in view for long stretches. Between Penmaenmawr and Llanfairfechan there is even a section where the line runs on a viaduct above the beach and in this picture, which was taken from an unusual viewpoint on the road overlooking the line, 'Royal Scot' Class 7P 4-6-0 No.46114 *Coldstream Guardsman* races across the structure with an unidentified up express in May 1962. *John Spencer Gilks*

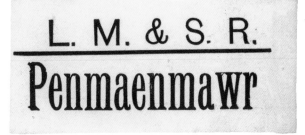

Bangor station occupies a compact site, sandwiched between Bangor tunnel to the east and Belmont tunnel to the west, and the passenger station, goods warehouse, motive power depot and civil engineers' department building had to be crammed into a restricted space. This panoramic picture shows virtually all of Bangor's railway installations, the only exception being the sizeable civil engineering depot (out of view to the right) which was responsible for the maintenance of two tubular bridges and lengthy exposed stretches of coastline. Bangor was the terminus of the line from Chester for two years while work on the Britannia bridge continued and almost as soon as the line to Holyhead opened the layout was the source of much criticism, but the situation was eased when, in 1881, authority was obtained to open out 135 yards of Belmont tunnel and, in addition, a road at the east end of the station was widened thus allowing the up platform to be later extended. Even so, in 1923 the station facilities still consisted of only two through platform lines, two fast tracks and two bays at the west end. The LMSR recognised that this was totally inadequate and implemented plans for an enlargement which was finished in 1927. This involved improving the operational flexibility of the station by laying up and down passenger and goods loops, plus considerable enhancements to the passenger amenities which included longer platform canopies. This shot, which was taken from above Belmont tunnel in August 1961, reveals that the station had changed little since the comprehensive rebuilding in the 1920s, except for the fact that the engine shed had been given a new roof at some stage. *Edwin Wilmshurst*

Compared to the previous illustration, Bangor shed (top left) seems as though it has suffered a mass exodus of its fleet, and indeed it had, being closed from 14th June 1965, just a month or so before this picture was taken. The shed, once a constant hive of activity both day and night, stands empty and the only locomotive on view is BR Standard Class 2MT 2-6-2T No.84009 which appears to be taking a rest during shunting operations. Most of Bangor's remaining allocation had been drafted to Llandudno Junction shed, No.84009's home depot. A July 1965 photograph. *Chris Evans*

The former Britannia tubular bridge across the Menai Strait was one of the marvels of the railway age and certainly the most impressive civil engineering achievement on the Chester to Holyhead line. Between 1818 and 1826 Thomas Telford's lofty single span suspension road bridge was erected across the Strait but those planning the railway bridge were not only obliged to meet the Admiralty's requirements for the uninterrupted passage of ships but also cater for the much heavier weight of railway locomotives and carriages. Robert Stephenson's design, which was decided upon in collaboration with William Fairbairn of Manchester, consisted of two wrought iron rectangular box sections through which each track would run and, most importantly, the weight of the riveted section of each tube (as they were known) had to be kept within the capacity of the hydraulic lifting jacks available at that time; three supporting towers were envisaged. Two of the towers were erected on land on each bank while the third, the Britannia tower, was built on a small rock island located roughly in the middle of the Strait, the latter tower rising around 200ft above the water. Each completed tube was 1,510ft long and supported by fixed bearings housed within the Britannia tower plus rollers in each land tower and the abutment at the ends. The total weight of the two tubes, including the track, supported by the three towers and two abutments, was estimated to be about 10,500 tons. The bridge was completed in 1850 but, regrettably, 120 years later this famous bridge suffered disastrous damage on the night of 23rd May 1970 when boys seeking birds' nests lit a paper torch which ignited rubbish, in turn setting fire to protective timbers and tar inside the tubes, the resultant conflagration being fanned by air currents. The extreme heat caused the wrought iron tubes to sag and the bridge was closed for rebuilding with rolling stock marooned on Anglesey being ferried across to the mainland by road. The structure was rebuilt with two steel arches and reopened on 30th January 1972 with a single running line only along the course of the former down line, the space formerly occupied by the up line being used for engineers' access. Between 1977 and 1980 a road bridge was constructed above the railway tracks and it is very unfortunate that the Egyptian stone lions, that had been such a hallmark of the structure, were hidden from view by the massive approach roads. In this view, taken on a sunny 24th May 1962, Stanier Class 5MT No.45144 emerges from the Britannia bridge with an up goods working; note that daylight is visible at the far end of the down line tube. Incessant road traffic now roars along where the photographer once stood, so another picture from the same viewpoint would be impossible. Note that one of the lions appears to be perched on the roof of the first van!
John Spencer Gilks

Holyhead, terminus of the North Wales Coast Line and 264 miles from Euston, has an unusual layout even for a maritime terminal. Its principal purpose has always been as a railhead for the boat traffic to and from the port of Dun Laoghaire in the Republic of Ireland. The original interchange facilities had never been particularly satisfactory, with passengers having to be transferred by horse-drawn carriages from the earlier stations, so when the present terminus was completed in 1880 it was built as conveniently as possible for the newly extended harbour. This has resulted in an unorthodox layout as it follows the harbour in the shape of a 'V', with a hotel separating the two arms of the station, the arrangement having the distinct advantage of providing a very short and easy interchange for travellers transferring between train and ship. Being completely covered it also offers some protection from the elements at an otherwise very exposed location. Goods facilities, both for general merchandise and the important Irish meat and cattle traffic were provided farther along the 'arms' of the pier. The left 'arm', with a single platform, was generally used for arriving trains and the right 'arm', with two platforms, for departures. This picture, which dates from July 1965, shows Platform 3 with a pair of Fowler 'Jinty' 0-6-0Ts fussing about on station pilot duty, whilst a Stanier Class 5MT 4-6-0 backs down to head for the shed after bringing in one of the relatively few passenger trains not timetabled to connect with a sailing. *Chris Evans*

When the first sod of the Conway & Llanrwst Railway (C&LR) was cut near Llanrwst on 25th August 1860 few of the gathered multitude at the ceremony would have anticipated that the line would eventually penetrate deep into the mountains of Snowdonia and reach Blaenau Festiniog. In 1863 the C&LR was swallowed up by the LNWR and on 17th June of that year the first passenger train left Llandudno at 1.30pm, the initial service being three trains in each direction on weekdays. In July 1875 the LNWR was authorised to extend the line to Betws-y-Coed and passenger trains commenced on 6th April 1868. The LNWR had its eye on the buoyant slate traffic originating at Blaenau Festiniog and, despite the cosy relationship the Festiniog Railway had with the Welsh Slate Company, decided to press on to Blaenau which proved a costly exercise. South of Betws-y-Coed the line was projected to climb steeply through the Lledr Valley before swinging southwards to enter a very long tunnel beneath the mountains. Hand boring of the tunnel started in January 1874, work being focussed at first on the northern end, and four shafts were excavated. The work involved blasting through hard rock and to add to the navvies' misery, at one point there was severe flooding; sadly some men lost their lives as a result of the arduous work and poor conditions. Despite these setbacks it was a momentous day when, on 4th April 1878, communication was achieved throughout the entire 3,861 yards-long tunnel. The extension was opened to a temporary station at Blaenau on 22nd July 1879, the permanent station opening in April 1881. Betws-y-Coed is the largest intermediate town on the line and the sturdily-built main station building is seen in this picture which dates from the 1950s. *Stuart Ackley collection*

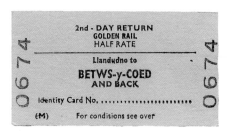

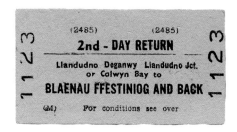

Blaenau Festiniog – a unique town surrounded by huge, man-made mountains of slate. The author was delighted when this picture was submitted for use in this album because colour photographs of BR steam in ordinary traffic on the Llandudno to Blaenau Festiniog line are extremely elusive. The latter town is often soaked in rain or shrouded in mist, so no doubt shots taken in the kind of bright and sunny conditions seen here are even harder to find. In this illustration Ivatt Class 2MT 2-6-2T No.41244 poses at Blaenau Festiniog on 16th July 1964 with, presumably, one of the pick-up goods trains from Llandudno Junction. This was the former North station, the old GWR Central station, which was served by trains from Bala Junction, having closed in early 1960. The Festiniog Railway narrow gauge line was partially operational at this time and was later opened throughout to Blaenau Festiniog, a town which has since undergone something of a renaissance. *Colin Caddy*

L. M. & S. R.
Blaenau Festiniog

In the 1860s the port of Amlwch had a population of 6,000 and this, plus the mineral deposits in the area, sparked interest among local entrepreneurs who wished to connect the port to the Chester & Holyhead Railway at Gaerwen. Various schemes proposed in the 1850s came to nought but on 13th July 1863 the promoters of the Anglesey Central Railway obtained an Act to build the 17¾ miles-long line and the first section from Gaerwen opened amid much celebration as far as Llangefni on 12th March 1865. On 1st February 1866 a further stretch was brought into use as far as Llanerchymedd, while the last, and final, section to Amlwch opened to passengers on 3rd June 1867. The LNWR purchased the local company in 1876 for £80,000. Six trains per weekday were scheduled in 1880 and this figure appears to have remained remarkably constant throughout the life of the line; latterly some trains ran to and from Bangor. The line was closed to passenger traffic from 7th December 1964 and this picture shows Ivatt Class 2MT 2-6-2T No.41226 reversing back into Amlwch station on 4th August 1964. The train had probably been shunted out of the station to enable No.41226 to take water and this may explain the presence of the fireman on the buffer beam. *J.W.T. House / Colin Caddy collection*

Table 89—   BANGOR, GAERWEN AND AMLWCH—Weekdays only.

Extract from London Midland Region winter 1959–60 timetable

The line from Bangor to Afon Wen was originally promoted by two separate companies and the first stretch was opened by the Bangor & Caernarvon Railway (B&CR) who obtained an Act on 20th May 1851 to build a railway to connect the towns. The line opened to passengers on 1st July 1852, the only major engineering work being the 497 yards-long Vaynol tunnel. The initial train service consisted of four weekday trains in each direction. In 1861 the Carnarvonshire Railway (CR) promoted a bill for a link between Pant, just south of Caernarvon, and Afon Wen, on the line from Dovey Junction to Pwllheli, and this received the Royal assent on 29th July 1862. The CR was partly built upon the formation of the Nantlle tramroad, the history of which can be traced back to 1828; the CR opened for business on 2nd September 1867. In 1870 the CR and B&CR were connected when, under the auspices of the LNWR, a link was laid in Caernarvon unifying the two lines. This picture shows a pick-up goods train, headed by Stanier Class 4MT 2-6-4T No.42601, at the former Dinas Junction station on 22nd May 1962. In bygone days this was a reasonably busy spot where goods were transhipped to the North Wales Narrow Gauge Railway (NWNGR); in the summer months there was also some passenger traffic. This line, opened in 1877, was very gradually extended with Portmadoc being reached in 1923. Traffic, however, was woefully thin and the Welsh Highland Light Railway, which had absorbed the NWNGR in 1922, ceased operations in 1937 thus ending Dinas Junction's status as a junction station. The days when standard and narrow gauge trains stood side by side in the station were well and truly over, and Dinas Junction's name was abbreviated to simply 'Dinas' in 1938; the station closed completely from 10th September 1951. Today, the narrow gauge Welsh Highland Railway runs from Caernarvon to Portmadoc and utilises part of the former standard gauge trackbed north of Dinas. *John Spencer Gilks*

The first plans for a railway connecting Bala with Blaenau Festiniog were promoted in 1865 but were abandoned due to the high construction costs. In 1873 the Bala and Festiniog Railway, backed by the GWR, obtained an Act to build the line and construction of the 22 miles-long line went ahead and was completed by 1882. There were 57 bridges on the route and no fewer than 16 viaducts so this probably explains why construction took so long. The largest viaduct, consisting of nine arches, carried the line 105 feet above the infant waters of Afon Prysor so there were clearly some quite massive civil engineering works involved. The line was opened throughout on 1st November 1882. Northbound trains on the Blaenau Festiniog branch commenced their journey at Bala Junction station which was purely an interchange point with the Ruabon to Barmouth Junction line and without road access. In this photograph, taken on a bright 28th August 1959, 7400 Class 0-6-0PT No.7443 awaits departure from Bala Junction with a one-coach branch train. The year 1959 was the last full year of operation along the entire branch, passenger services north of Bala being withdrawn from 4th January 1960 so they only just survived into the following year. Services between Bala Junction and Bala lasted longer, being withdrawn from 18th January 1965 when the Ruabon to Barmouth route was closed. *Roy Denison*

A shuttle service operated between Bala and Bala Junction and while the appropriate arrival and departure times to/from Bala for connections with 'main line' trains at Bala Junction were listed in the timetable; confusingly the latter station was not mentioned in the Barmouth to Ruabon line tables. Instead that timetable stated in the footnotes that 'Passengers to and from Bala change at Bala Junction by most of the trains', which hinted that it was something of a lottery. One wonders whether any passengers were ever stranded at Bala Junction, a station that did not have any road access. Here No.7443 pauses at Bala with the train seen in the previous picture. *Roy Denison*

(65712)	(65712)
2nd-SINGLE	SINGLE-2nd
Bala Junction to	
Bala Junction	Bala Junction
Bala	Bala
BALA	
(M) 0/3	Fare 0/3 (M)
For conditions see over	For conditions see over

6539   6539

The scenery on some sections of the Bala Junction to Blaenau Festiniog line was similar to that found on the wilder stretches of the West Highland and Settle to Carlisle lines. Here a northbound goods train is surrounded by bare moorland as it ascends an incline near Cwm Prysor in May 1958. Motive power is provided by 8750 Class 0-6-0PT No.4617 which was nominally allocated to Croes Newydd shed near Wrexham. It is likely, however, that this locomotive spent a considerable time away from its home depot working from sub-sheds at Bala, Trawsfynydd or Penmaenpool. *John Spencer Gilks*

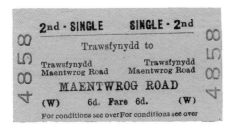

The 9.15am Blaenau Festiniog to Bala Junction train, formed of a single coach, is seen near Cwm Prysor on May 13th 1958 with 5800 Class 0-4-2T No.5810 in charge; note the platelayers' trolley on the left of the shot. The rugged and inhospitable landscape on this particular section of line was quite dramatic and near Arenig the line passed Arenig Fawr, the peak of which is 2,800 feet above sea level. The summit of the line (1,278 feet above sea level) was reached at Cwm Prysor and from there the line descended towards Trawsfynydd along a series of ledges and cuttings that had been carved out of the mountainside: the course of the line is just visible in the distance. No.5810 was one of a small class of twenty 0-4-2Ts built in 1933 for light branch line work but, unlike their 1400 Class sister engines, they were not fitted for auto train operation. *John Spencer Gilks*

Trawsfynydd is only a village but the name will strike a chord with many readers because it is the site of a nuclear power station and also Llyn Trawsfynydd, a large reservoir. In this picture 7400 Class 0-6-0PT No.7414 is seen taking water at Trawsfynydd station in the course of working a short goods train from Bala to Blaenau Festiniog in May 1958. There are no fewer than eight gentlemen on the platform of whom four are railwaymen in uniform while another two are clearly the engine crew. Surely the remaining two men were not waiting for a train – perhaps they were the local platelayers. When this line was closed a new connection was installed between Blaenau Festiniog North (LMR) and Central (WR) stations to provide access to the new power station. *John Spencer Gilks*

Rather than state that Maentwrog Road was a small station with a huge nameboard one is tempted to say that the huge nameboard had a small station attached! One wonders how many people alighted at Maentwrog Road and walked the, no doubt, very hilly three miles to Tan-y-Bwlch. This shot was taken on a very gloomy 20th June 1959. *John Langford*

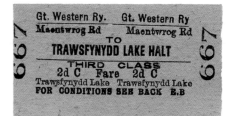

A busy scene at Festiniog station in May 1958 as 7400 Class 0-6-0PT No.7414, hauling a goods train bound for Blaenau Festiniog, waits in the platform while sister engine No.7442 comes off the single line section with a southbound goods working. In the background low cloud conceals a mountain top. *John Spencer Gilks*

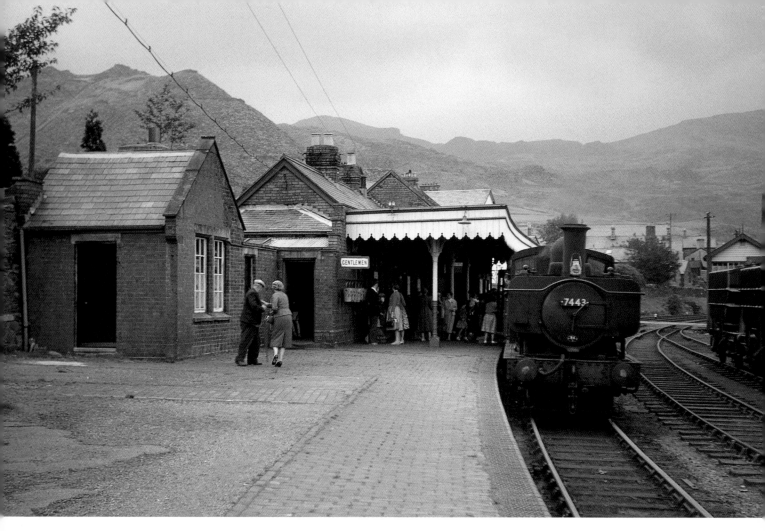

The 'mountains' of slate provide an unmistakable backdrop to this picture of Blaenau Festiniog Central station on 28th August 1959 which shows 7400 Class 0-6-0PT No.7443 simmering in the platform after arrival with a train from Bala. A fair number of passengers appear to have alighted from the train but, even so, the line was closed to passenger traffic, as previously mentioned, just over four months later. The 1954/55 winter timetable advertised only three weekday trains in each direction along the full length of the line but, in addition, there were extra trains on Saturdays while, for reasons unknown to the author, one train ran on Tuesdays, Thursdays and Saturdays only. One particularly interesting service was the 10.25pm from Blaenau Festiniog, which was a short working which ran only as far as Trawsfynydd, presumably for the benefit of Saturday night revellers who had been letting their hair down in Blaenau. The mind boggles! *Roy Denison*

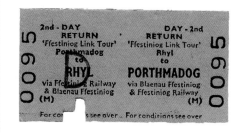

Extract from Western Region winter 1953–54 timetable

Like so many lines, the Ruabon to Barmouth Junction route was developed piecemeal and several separate companies were involved. The Vale of Llangollen Railway obtained an Act on 1st August 1859 to construct the 5¼ miles-long section from Ruabon, on the Chester to Shrewsbury route, to Llangollen and this was brought into use on 2nd June 1862. The Llangollen & Corwen Railway was authorised in 1860 and opened on 8th May 1865; two viaducts were built and a 686 yards-long tunnel bored during its construction. The stretch of line from Corwen on to Bala was opened throughout by the Corwen & Bala Railway on 1st April 1868. The Bala & Dolgelly Railway (B&DR) had obtained an Act in 1863 authorising construction of its 17¼ miles-long line between the two towns and this opened on 4th August 1868. This picturesque section ran alongside Bala lake for 3½ miles and beyond the lake reached the 760 feet-high summit of the Ruabon to Barmouth line at Garneddwen before descending to Dolgelly. There the B&DR met the Cambrian Railways' line from Barmouth which had originally been planned by the Aberystwyth & Welch Coast Railway but this did not open to passengers until 11th June 1869. This shot is one of a series of colour pictures taken by the photographer during the course of a journey from Wrexham to Pwllheli on Saturday 20th June 1959. His train was double-headed by 4300 Class 'Moguls' Nos.7310 and 6357 from Wrexham to Barmouth Junction and the line beyond Ruabon was quite busy, bearing in mind that the main holiday season had not yet started. Between Ruabon and Barmouth his train crossed four other services heading eastwards including 5700 Class 0-6-0PT No.5774, on the 7.12am Bala to Birkenhead train, which is seen here approaching Glyndyfrdwy. Originally there was no passing loop at this location, but in 1877 another platform was constructed and a second line laid thus enabling two trains to cross. *John Langford*

The line between Llangollen and Corwen was opened for business in May 1865 and closed from 18th January 1965 so it just missed achieving its centenary. In this relatively rare picture of a goods train on the Ruabon to Barmouth line 4300 Class 2-6-0 No.6306 stands in Corwen station with (what appears to be) a local pick-up working. Trains of this nature once played a huge role in the operation of the railway, stopping at wayside stations to shunt goods yards and set down or pick up wagons as necessary – an aspect of operation long since consigned to history. Note that the station building is constructed of local stone and no two blocks appear to be the same. Note also the scissors crossing just beyond the ends of the platforms, a most unusual feature at a quiet country station. The track on the left is the former LNWR line to Rhyl while the 'main line' to Ruabon is on the right. The former route was closed to regular passenger traffic in February 1953 but remained *in situ* for excursion trains until 8th September 1961. *Edwin Wilmshurst*

RUABON TO MORFA MAWDDACH (BARMOUTH JUNCTION)

This is another photograph taken on 20th June 1959 by the enthusiast referred to in a previous caption. On arrival at Bala Junction he found two other trains in the station, 4300 Class 2-6-0 No.7313 on the 7.20am from Barmouth to Wrexham and an unidentified pannier tank locomotive which was simmering near the signal box (on the extreme right of the picture) no doubt after bringing in a shuttle service from Bala. The existence of Bala Junction station was only grudgingly acknowledged in the BR public timetable (as previously mentioned) because it was listed in the index at the front but did not appear in the table listing Ruabon to Barmouth services. A footnote merely advised passengers to and from Bala to change at Bala Junction station. *John Langford*

Photographed on a bright and sunny autumn day, BR Standard Class 4MT 4-6-0 No.75006 pauses at Drws-y-Nant with an unidentified eastbound train, probably the 10.20am Barmouth to Ruabon, on 3rd October 1964. When the line was first built there was only a single platform here but as a result of increasing traffic a second platform and passing loop were provided in 1895. In the summer 1961 timetable the train service along the route consisted of five local services in each direction supplemented by some short workings, mainly to and from Bala. In addition, there were Saturdays-only holiday services, one of which, the 9.00am from Paddington to Pwllheli, ran non-stop from Ruabon to Morfa Mawddach (formerly Barmouth Junction). This train even conveyed a restaurant car as far as Barmouth but this unaccustomed luxury was not, of course, available to local passengers. Like so many lines that were worked to capacity on summer Saturdays, all-year-round local passenger traffic was insufficient to stave off closure and the last normal passenger trains were withdrawn from this very scenic route on 18th January 1965. It should be noted, however, that the Llangollen to Bala Junction section was prematurely closed by flooding from 13th December 1964 and a substitute bus service provided until the official closure date. *J.W.T. House / Colin Caddy collection*

Bontnewydd station was most unusual because one platform had been constructed with brick facing and coping stones in the traditional manner while the other one was built of wood, which suggests that it may have been a wartime addition when a passing loop was installed. The signal box, visible on the right, controlled a level crossing on a country lane. Like most of the wayside stations on this line, Bontnewydd served little more than a few cottages so passenger receipts were probably miniscule. This shot of BR Standard Class 4MT No.75029 in charge of a westbound train, possibly the 9.27am Ruabon to Barmouth, was taken on 3rd October 1964. *J.W.T. House / Colin Caddy collection*

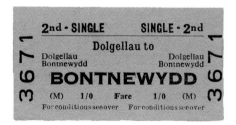

RUABON TO MORFA MAWDDACH (BARMOUTH JUNCTION)

An eastbound train, headed by BR Standard Class 4MT No.75006, enters Penmaenpool station on 3rd October 1964. The station was approached from the north by a wooden trestle toll bridge, partially visible on the right, across the Mawddach estuary, the station site being hemmed in by the river on one side and the main road to Dolgelly on the other. Despite the restricted space a small two-road engine shed was built west of the station, this being a sub-shed of Croes Newydd (Wrexham) depot. *J.W.T. House / Colin Caddy collection*

BR Standard Class 4MT No.75021 and Ivatt Class 2MT No.46521 stand outside the small shed at Penmaenpool on 24th May 1964; the 'main line' track is in the foreground. The Bala & Dolgelly Railway opened in August 1868 and for a time Dolgelly was a terminal station until the Cambrian Railways' line from Barmouth Junction reached the town during the following year, the opening date being 11th June 1869. The Cambrian decided to construct an engine shed at Penmaenpool and this also opened in 1869. It was a tiny two-road affair but presumably was more than adequate on this lightly trafficked route; the shed was closed in January 1965. *Colin Caddy*

Between Dolgelly and Penmaenpool the railway entered the unspoilt estuary of the river Mawddach, which is widely regarded as one of the most attractive in Great Britain, and ran within sight of the river for the next few miles to Barmouth. The journey from Ruabon was characterised by tree-covered, steep sided gorges, tumbling rivers plus, of course, the delightful panorama across Bala lake, but none of these surpassed the Mawddach estuary's serene beauty which was one of the undoubted highlights of the Ruabon to Barmouth route. Unfortunately, on the day that this picture was taken the dull weather conditions were not conducive to railway photography but, even so, this shot gives at least a hint of the scenic splendours of this section of line. This photograph was taken near Arthog station, located a mile or so east of Morfa Mawddach, and depicts an unidentified summer Saturday holiday working with former GWR 'Mogul' No.6375 in charge. Let us hope the weather improved for the holiday-makers. This picture was taken on 14th July 1962. *John Langford*

RUABON TO MORFA MAWDDACH (BARMOUTH JUNCTION)

The Shrewsbury to Aberystwyth line crosses the Welsh border at Middletown, about five miles east of Welshpool, and runs alongside the river Severn for a short distance. The 'Cambrian Coast Express' was undoubtedly the best-known train serving mid-Wales and in this picture a gleaming 'Manor' Class 4-6-0 No.7823 *Hook Norton Manor* stands in Welshpool station on 31st March 1962. The 'Manor' would have taken over at Shrewsbury, where the train reversed, and worked through to Aberystwyth, a distance of 81½ miles. The history of the 'Cambrian Coast Express' can be traced back to 1927 when it was introduced by the GWR. When this picture was taken Welshpool was still a relatively thriving railway centre with a local 'all stations' service to Shrewsbury and trains to Oswestry and Whitchurch along the former main line of the Cambrian Railways. The closure of the latter route in November 1964 heralded a downturn in the fortunes of Welshpool station and today the impressive French Renaissance style station building, which was once the headquarters of the Oswestry & Newtown Railway, no longer functions as railway premises, being in commercial use, and trains now stop at a new station on a different site. *Hugh Ballantyne*

An unidentified eastbound local train, headed by BR Standard Class 4MT 2-6-4T No.80132, in quite clean condition, crosses the river Severn near Newtown on 8th August 1964. By the date of this picture around a dozen of these locomotives had been drafted to Croes Newydd (Wrexham), Oswestry and Shrewsbury sheds and were, for a brief period, a regular sight on the Cambrian main line on stopping passenger trains; this particular example was based at Oswestry. The summer 1962 timetable reveals a total of seven stopping trains in each direction between Machynlleth and Welshpool, some of which went to Shrewsbury while others served Oswestry and Whitchurch. The service to Whitchurch was withdrawn in January 1965 while six months later a complete revision of services along the Cambrian main line took place following the withdrawal of stopping trains and the closure of many intermediate stations. *Martin Smith*

The Shrewsbury to Aberystwyth line was opened throughout by the mid-1860s but that statement hides the fact that various local concerns were involved in the route's construction and some faced very difficult, inhospitable terrain and bad weather conditions. The first part of this line to be brought into use was the short section from (what later became) Moat Lane Junction to Newtown which was constructed by the Llanidloes & Newtown Railway and opened on 2nd September 1859. The Welshpool to Newtown stretch, which was promoted by the Oswestry and Newtown Railway, was brought into use on 10th June 1861 and it is recorded that most services continued from Newtown to Llanidloes. The line connecting Shrewsbury to Welshpool was built by a company of that name who obtained an Act on 29th July 1856; the line opened on 27th January 1862. Of all the companies involved in building the Shrewsbury to Aberystwyth route, the Newtown & Machynlleth Railway undoubtedly faced the biggest natural obstacles and at times harsh weather conditions. The route westwards from Newtown was along the Garno valley and over Talerddig summit where it crossed the watershed of the Severn and Dovey rivers. A 120 feet-deep cutting at Talerddig was for a time the deepest railway cutting in the world. The first contractor's train reached Machynlleth on May Day 1862 and the route was fully opened on 3rd January 1863. The Aberystwyth & Welch Coast Railway obtained an Act on 22nd July 1861 to build a line from Aberystwyth to Pwllheli with a link to Machynlleth and the section of line linking Machynlleth to Aberystwyth was commissioned on 23rd June 1864. This picture, taken on 4th August 1962, depicts Moat Lane Junction station and shows a 'Manor' 4-6-0, No.7802 *Bradley Manor* awaiting departure with an eastbound train, while a couple of Ivatt Class 2MT locomotives are visible on the right of the shot. Moat Lane was the junction for the Three Cocks and Brecon line and trains on that route left from another platform on the other side of the station building. This was once an interesting country junction but, sadly, today virtually no trace of the station remains. *Edwin Wilmshurst*

G. W. R.

Moat Lane

Via MERTHYR & TALYLLYN

'Moat Lane Junction, change for Llanidloes, Rhayader, Builth Wells, Brecon and South Wales' proclaims the comprehensive nameboard on the eastbound platform. Changing at Moat Lane may have been the ideal option for railway aficionados heading for South Wales, the trip to Brecon along the former Mid Wales Railway being breathtakingly beautiful and full of railway interest, but the journey to Newport, for example, on the 9.55am from Moat Lane would have occupied no less than 6½ hours, including a long wait at Brecon for a southbound connection, so for most travellers a change of trains at Shrewsbury would have been preferable. At least the sojourn at Brecon coincided with lunchtime – perhaps the timetable planners intended it that way! In this early 1960s view there are three locomotives visible, two in the immediate station area and a third can just be discerned behind the wagons near the engine shed which was a sub-shed of Oswestry. A shed was provided at Moat Lane Junction when the line from Newtown to Llanidloes opened in 1859 and this wooden structure lasted until a brand new corrugated building was constructed in 1957. Clearly at that time BR had not contemplated closure of the lightly-trafficked rural line to Brecon and took the view that investment in a new shed was justified but, sadly, it only survived five years in railway use, closing at the end of December 1962. *Stuart Ackley collection*

Most of the wayside stations between Shrewsbury and Aberystwyth fell victim to the Beeching axe, no fewer than fourteen being closed from 14th June 1965; some of the buildings are still extant, however, in private ownership. The elimination of those stations permitted a recast of the timetable and overall journey times were reduced by up to 40 minutes. Carno station, between Caersws and Machynlleth, served no more than a church, public house and a few cottages so its demise is probably not too surprising, especially as it was on the main road between those places. This view, looking south-eastwards, of the pleasant little station at Carno was taken in 1964, the last full year of its existence. The main building there, built of stone laid in a delightful higgledy-piggledy fashion, was almost identical to that at Llanbrynmair, the next station down the line after Talerddig. The level crossing carried a minor road across the tracks. *Stuart Ackley collection*

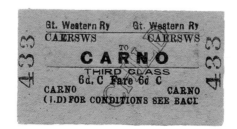

Many a locomotive fireman must have breathed a huge sigh of relief when Talerddig station hove into view after a gruelling climb from either Newtown or Machynlleth. Sometimes up trains stopped there to permit a pilot engine to be uncoupled, the locomotive returning to Machynlleth. The climb for westbound trains was fairly moderate, the worst section being the 1 in 80 gradient for the last mile up to the summit at Talerddig station which was situated 693 feet above sea level. It was a different story for eastbound trains, however, which were faced with 15 miles of almost continuous climbing from Machynlleth, the final section from Llanbrynmair on gradients as steep as 1 in 52/56. Note the oil lamps and that the small station has a full set of regulation fire buckets. The waiting shelter on the down side appears to have suffered from subsidence – perhaps the local rabbit population had something to answer for! This portrait of Talerddig station dates from 1964. *Stuart Ackley collection*

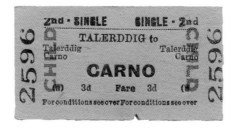

Almost in sight of the summit. Between Newtown and Machynlleth a main road follows the course of the railway and near Talerddig they are within a few feet of each other, so it would have been possible for car-bound enthusiasts to photograph a slow-moving train near Llanbrynmair and take another picture just before Talerddig station – at least in theory! In this picture 4300 Class 2-6-0 No.6368 heaves a nine-coach eastbound train up the 1 in 56 towards the summit on 27th July 1963 and one can only imagine the deafening blast from this machine which was probably working to its limit. No.6368 was built at Swindon works, emerging in October 1925, and lasted in traffic until withdrawn five months after this shot was taken. *John Spencer Gilks*

Photographed at the same location as the previous picture, the up 'Cambrian Coast Express' is seen with two very neglected BR Standard Class 4MT 4-6-0s in charge on 9th July 1966. The locomotives are Nos.75013 and 75016 and, despite their disgraceful external condition, they appear to be romping up to the summit with their nine-coach load. Could the photographer have wished for a more spectacular smoke effect? *Colin Caddy*

SHREWSBURY TO MACHYNLLETH

Normally steam locomotives ascending the 1 in 52/56 incline up to Talerddig station produced a lot of smoke and steam, much to the delight of lineside enthusiasts, but on this occasion the photographer must have been a trifle disappointed as 2251 Class 0-6-0 No.3200 trundled past his vantage point almost effortlessly – or so it seems. This scene was recorded in the summer of 1956 and depicts a pick-up goods train. These slow-moving trains (as previously mentioned) stopped at wayside stations to pick up or set down wagons as required which invariably involved a little bit of shunting. Note the particularly neat permanent way, a legacy of the days when maintenance of each length of track was the responsibility of a specific gang who took pride in the appearance of their 'length'. *Colin Hogg*

Most of the really hard work is over for the crew of 'Manor' 4-6-0 No.7827 *Lydham Manor*, in charge of the westbound 'Cambrian Coast Express', which is seen drifting down the 1 in 52 gradient into Llanbrynmair station on 8th August 1964. In WR days the locomotive hauling this train would have been absolutely immaculate but by the date of this picture standards were obviously starting to slip – at least the engine's nameplates are still attached. Designed by the GWR, the first 'Manor' took to the rails in early 1938 but *Lydham Manor* was one of ten constructed after the Second World War, not entering service until December 1950. *Martin Smith*

Locomotive crews working eastbound trains on the Cambrian main line were probably none too pleased when they reached Llanbrynmair because this station marked the start of the heavy gradients up to Talerddig summit and really hard work for the firemen. The grades from Machynlleth were relatively moderate, the worst stretch being a short section of 1 in 60, but after leaving Llanbrynmair there was an unrelenting climb, mainly at 1 in 52, until the summit was reached. This picture gives no indication of the demanding nature of this line because Llanbrynmair station just happened to occupy the only level stretch on the climb! This illustration shows the eastbound platform with its rather rudimentary waiting shelter and tiny signal box. Llanbrynmair was a vital crossing point for trains on the single line and the signalman there was doubtless fully occupied on busy summer Saturdays, but if trains were held up there at least the passengers could get out and admire the wonderful scenery at this location.
Martin Smith

G. W. R.

LLANBRYNMAIR

Variety at Commins Coch. A brace of 'Dukedog' 4-4-0s, the leading engine is No.9012, battle their way up to Talerddig during the summer of 1956. A total of 29 of these locomotives was assembled between 1936-39 using boilers from withdrawn 'Duke' class engines and the outside frames from the 'Bulldog' class, hence the name 'Dukedog'. The class was intended to be named after earls and the first twelve were fitted with nameplates, but the GWR received complaints from some earls who objected to their names being carried by such antiquated-looking machines and to placate them the names were quickly transferred to the much more impressive looking 'Castle' class express passenger locomotives. By the time of this picture twenty of these 'Dukedog' locomotives remained in service but in 1957 a major cull took place and the class was reduced to just seven representatives by the end of that year. The last survivors were Nos. 9014 and 9017, both of which were withdrawn in October 1960. *Colin Hogg*

A 'Manor' Class 4-6-0 pilots a BR Standard Class 4MT 4-6-0 past Commins Coch in July 1963. There is barely a trace of smoke from either locomotive's chimney – the trademark of skilled firemen. There used to be a station at Commins Coch, which was described in the public timetable as a 'halt', but despite this description nearly all local trains on the line were booked to stop. The gradient at this point is a relatively moderate 1 in 113 and much sterner work lay ahead of the crew after Llanbrynmair. *John Spencer Gilks*

2nd-SINGLE SINGLE-2nd

Cemmes Road to

| Cemmes Road | Cemmes Road |
| Commins Coch Ht | Commins Coch Ht |

COMMINS COCH HALT

(W)   5d. Fare 5d.   (W)

For conditions see over For conditions see over

0577   0577

The fireman of BR Standard Class 4MT 2-6-4T No.80099 may not have employed the firing technique suggested in the BR manual but at least the volcanic smoke effect being emitted by his locomotive produced a memorable photograph when it passed Commins Coch with an eastbound stopping train in July 1963. Out-shopped from Brighton works in January 1955, No.80099 spent the greater part of its short BR career at Plaistow shed, east London, for working services on the Fenchurch Street to Shoeburyness line. When this route was electrified in the early 1960s No.80099 was transferred to Swansea but by 1963 was based at Croes Newydd shed at Wrexham. It was later allocated to Machynlleth from where it was withdrawn in May 1965. *John Spencer Gilks*

The long 6½-hour journey from London to the Welsh coast is almost over for passengers aboard the down 'Cambrian Coast Express' which is depicted here entering Machynlleth behind 'Manor' Class 4-6-0 No.7823 *Hook Norton Manor* on 16th July 1962. Judging by its pristine condition this locomotive was clearly the pride of Aberystwyth shed at that time. Note that the vehicle immediately behind the locomotive has its fifth compartment window blanked out of use. This coach is almost certainly second class corridor carriage No.W25189 which had been experimentally equipped with (what BR described as) an auto buffet that enabled passengers to obtain snacks after the manned refreshment car had been detached. Sadly, this brave venture was not perpetuated because the coach's vibration affected the machine's delicate mechanism. In the early 1960s the future of rail services to mid-Wales was being considered and it was decided to concentrate as much traffic as possible on the Shrewsbury to Aberystwyth route at the expense of the Ruabon to Barmouth, Afon Wen and Carmarthen lines which were

scheduled for closure. There was modest investment at Machynlleth to accommodate the anticipated additional business: note the new building in the foreground which was built to handle goods traffic previously dealt with by various smaller depots earmarked for closure and covered a wide area of mid-Wales. Note also that the new premises have been kitted out with a generous supply of fire buckets, just in case! The somewhat older, soot-blackened motive power depot is immediately behind the goods shed. *Rodney Lissenden*

A scene at Machynlleth shed taken in June 1963 showing BR Standard Class 3MT 2-6-2T No.82034 in green livery posing in the sunshine while BR 4-6-0 No.75004 lurks in the shed. Released from Swindon works in January 1955, No.82034 was initially allocated to Newton Abbot depot but later moved to Chester. By April 1961 it was based at Machynlleth and was destined to stay for a number of years before being transferred to Patricroft shed, near Manchester, from where it was withdrawn in December 1966. The former Cambrian Railways' shed at Machynlleth, which occupied a very cramped site, was unusual in that it had three roads at the western end but only two at the other end; there was a 65-foot turntable positioned behind the photographer. Note the very close proximity of the hillside which no doubt had to be hacked away when the shed was built in 1863. The shed closed to steam in December 1966. *Alan Reeve*

A bird's-eye view of Machynlleth station in the early 1960s with the meandering river Dovey visible in the background. Sometimes described as *cottage orné*, the Newtown & Machynlleth Railway built a set of stations in this style, of which Machynlleth is the largest. Constructed of local stone in 1863 the building is two storeys high with three prominent gables, decorative bargeboards and finials. There is a train in the down platform with a 'Manor' Class locomotive at its head while an Ivatt Class 2MT engine stands on the adjacent road. The separate building to the left of the main building is presumably the stationmaster's house. The amount of land available for railway installations was at a premium at Machynlleth and in the foreground on the left is (what appears to be) the cattle dock which has been squeezed in between the station and much higher ground from where this shot was taken. *Stuart Ackley collection*

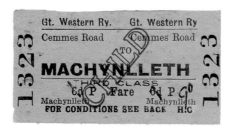

A further illustration of Machynlleth from a high position but this time looking north-eastwards. The most prominent structures in the foreground are the coaling plant with the locomotive shed beyond and, to the left of the 'coaler', the goods distribution depot built following the decision to concentrate all traffic to and from mid-Wales on the Shrewsbury to Aberystwyth line. The main line tracks separate the shed from the goods yard which contains a breakdown vehicle in red livery. Beyond the goods yard is the site of the exchange sidings with the erstwhile Corris Railway which carried slate from quarries at Aberllefenni to Machynlleth; the trackbed of the former narrow gauge line, which ran across the fields in the background, can just be discerned. The line opened on 30th April 1859, thus becoming the first railway to serve Machynlleth, but passenger services ceased in 1931 shortly after it was acquired by the GWR. In 1948 the line was affected by flooding, closing from 20th August of that year, and it had been dismantled by 1950. *Stuart Ackley collection*

G. W. R.

MACHYNLLETH

Pictured in the attractive setting of Dovey Junction station, 'Manor' Class 4-6-0 No.7819 *Hinton Manor* has arrived from Aberystwyth and awaits the arrival of the portion from Pwllheli on a sunny day in 1963. No.7819 is one of nine locomotives of this class to survive in preservation out of a total of 30 engines. *Alan Reeve*

G. W. R.

Dovey Junction

A station in the middle of nowhere. Constructed on an exposed marshland, Dovey Junction station was built solely to provide an interchange point between the Aberystwyth and Pwllheli routes and had no road access. This picture was taken from about half a mile away, looking westwards, on 6th August 1966 and shows the up 'Cambrian Coast Express' departing behind a BR Standard Class 4MT 4-6-0 – unsurprisingly the locomotive was not identified! The rather delicate-looking trestle bridge on the left of the photograph carries the Pwllheli line across the river Dovey, the estuary of which can be clearly seen on the right. *Trevor Owen / John Spencer Gilks collection*

The engine cleaners at Aberystwyth shed have just given 'Manor' Class 4-6-0 No.7828 *Odney Manor* a final polish prior to its working the up 'Cambrian Coast Express' and here it is seen backing down into the station which is just visible on the far right of the shot. What a splendid sight! A BR Standard 4-6-0 and 2-6-4T can be seen on the left but, alas, their external condition does not quite match the sparkle of *Odney Manor*. The building behind the locomotive is Aberystwyth shed which was only 25 years old when this picture was taken, having been constructed in 1938 as a replacement for the original depot, built way back in 1864. At this time the narrow gauge Vale of Rheidol Railway (VoR) had its own, separate shed but in 1968 VoR locomotive operations were transferred to the standard gauge shed which retained its 45,000 gallon capacity water tank, this being more than sufficient, presumably, for the three VoR locomotives! Aberystwyth has become one of the very last survivors of 400 former GWR steam sheds. This photograph was taken in August 1963. *Derek Penney*

A fascinating view of the extremely sinuous approach to Aberystwyth station from the Carmarthen line, with the motive power depot on the right with (what appears to be) a 4300 Class 2-6-0 standing outside. The 'main line' to Carmarthen is presumably the track in the foreground. One of the station platforms is just visible together with a nameboard; note the forest of semaphore signals. The sixteen-ton mineral wagon, on the extreme right, is on the elevated coaling plant siding. *Stuart Ackley collection*

When this portrait was taken of BR Standard Class 4MT 4-6-0 No.75048 waiting to leave Aberystwyth with the up 'Cambrian Coast Express' on 18th February 1967, steam traction had only a further two weeks to live on the route to Shrewsbury. The machine's paintwork hardly sparkles in the dull conditions but at least the locomotive was respectably clean and producing some smoke and steam for the photographer. Strangely, apart from one bystander, there is nobody on the platform so perhaps the engine was photographed well before departure time as it was simply heating the train. A fortnight later steam bowed out on the route when No.75033, which had been cleaned by photographers, powered the final up 'Cambrian Coast Express' while the last down train was worked by a very scruffy No.75021. When the GWR acquired the Cambrian Railways in 1923 the enlargement of Aberystwyth station, which had been inadequate to cope with the resort's holiday traffic, was top priority. Platforms were extended and the passenger facilities improved and modernised, but perhaps the most striking new feature was the new, two storey frontage block in white stone in Georgian style. The rebuilt premises were completed in 1924. *Graham Mallinson*

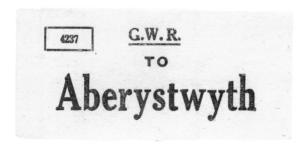

The late 1850s saw hotels springing up along Cardigan Bay at places such as Towyn and Barmouth and this, together with the belief that Port Dinllaen on the Lleyn peninsula might be developed for the Irish traffic, sparked interest in a railway to serve the port and the growing tourist potential. Various schemes were put forward and rejected, but the plans of the Aberystwyth & Welch Coast Railway (A&WCR) for a line from Aberystwyth to Pwllheli were accepted by Parliament and this company obtained an Act on 22nd July 1861; a short link from (what is now known as) Dovey Junction to Machynlleth was also proposed. A later Act authorised an extension from Pwllheli to Port Dinllaen but this was never implemented. Not surprisingly, the Aberystwth to Machynlleth section was the first to be built and this opened to passenger traffic on 23rd June 1864 with through trains from Whitchurch almost from the start. The A&WCR, rather than focus on the crossing of the River Dovey, then turned its attention to constructing the Aberdovey to Llwyngwril and Penmaenpool section which was partially opened on 3rd July 1865. The Dovey Junction to Aberdovey stretch, which involved constructing a 140 yards-long viaduct with a total of twenty spans across the river Dovey, opened on 14th August 1867. This section proved to be particularly challenging with four tunnels, heavy earthworks and sea walls at Aberdovey which took the line along a sinuous route behind the town. It is interesting to note that until the opening of Barmouth bridge passengers for Barmouth were faced with the stark choice of a detour via Dolgelly or taking a small boat across the estuary which, depending on the tide, involved a walk across the rough, pebbly beach! After many setbacks the outstandingly scenic Dovey Junction to Pwllheli line opened throughout on 10th October 1867. The scenic splendours of this line are amply illustrated here in this shot of BR Standard Class 3MT 2-6-2T No.82006 heading northwards between Dovey Junction and Aberdovey on a sunny 26th September 1964. The estuary of the river Dovey and distant mountains provide the perfect backdrop.
Martin Smith

During the last year or two of steam traction, operations were monopolised by BR Standard Class 4MTs and in this picture No.75002, working a Machynlleth-bound train, is seen near Gogarth Halt in September 1966. The halt was situated 1½ miles from Dovey junction, on the other side of the estuary, and was one of a number of halts on the line opened by the GWR in the 1920s. In the mid-1970s, however, it was washed away during severe flooding and officially closed from 3rd January 1976. *John Spencer Gilks*

A Pwllheli-bound train, headed by BR Standard Class 3MT 2-6-2T No.82000, is about to plunge into Penhelig tunnel on 26th May 1964. When it was constructed Penhelig tunnel was clearly not built with particularly generous clearances and one wonders how much space there was between No.82000's cab roof and that of the tunnel. The author was under the impression that locomotives of this class allocated to the WR were always painted green, but No.82000 was obviously an exception. This machine appears to have spent almost its entire working career on the Cambrian Lines, mostly based at Machynlleth: perhaps it was repainted in black livery during a works overhaul after Machynlleth shed came under LMR control in 1963. At least No.82000's paintwork is in a reasonable condition in contrast to that on the coach which is in an appalling state.
Colin Caddy

In August 1963 HM The Queen and HRH The Duke of Edinburgh visited the Outward Bound School at Aberdovey. Despite the overcast conditions two gleaming 'Manors' – Nos. 7827 *Lydham Manor* and 7828 *Odney Manor* – make a fine sight as they head northwards from Aberdovey with the empty stock of the Royal train in tow on 9th August. A total of four locomotives was specially prepared for Royal duty, the others being Nos. 7819 *Hinton Manor* and 7822 *Foxcote Manor,* and all four took a hand in hauling either the Royal train or its associated empty stock workings. It is interesting to note that while the Cambrian lines had been transferred from WR to LMR control in January 1963, locomotives of this class, rather than LMR or BR Standard types, were entrusted with the operation of these high-profile trains. *Derek Penney*

It is always a great honour for enginemen when they are selected for Royal train duty and here one of the crews involved with the Royal working to Aberdovey pose proudly beside the train, while another driver looks down from his cab. Unfortunately, the fourth crew member seems to have missed the opportunity to have his picture taken. *Derek Penney*

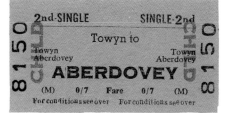

The 'Parcels Office and Cloak Room' sign on the extreme right, and gas lighting, suggests that this picture of Towyn station was taken back in steam days and indeed it was, being photographed on 16th July 1962; it shows the main station buildings on the up platform, looking northwards. Towyn is, of course, famous as the headquarters of the Talyllyn Railway, the pioneer of railway preservation in Great Britain and, as far as the author is aware, the rest of world. Quite an achievement! *Rodney Lissenden*

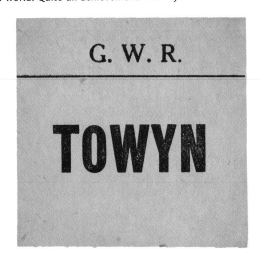

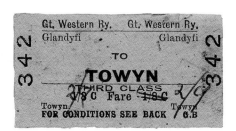

In 1870 the line at Friog cliffs, between Llwyngwril and Barmouth Junction, was threatened when rock, already suffering from erosion, was disturbed by a mine heading. It was suggested that a tunnel deviation was necessary but the Cambrian Railways baulked at the cost and nothing was done. This was a decision they lived to regret because on the night of 1st January 1883 an evening train from Machynlleth ran into a landslide, throwing the locomotive onto the rocks below and killing the crew. On 4th March 1933 a similar incident occurred at the same location when the morning mail train from Machynlleth struck fallen rocks; once again the locomotive was derailed, sent crashing down to the shore and the enginemen lost their lives. Following this second tragedy the GWR constructed a reinforced concrete avalanche shelter and buttresses were built on other sections of the cliff face. This picture of the avalanche shelter was taken from an approaching train in 1963. *Stuart Ackley collection*

An unidentified southbound passenger train, probably the up 'Cambrian Coast Express', hauled by BR Standard Class 4MT No.75009, is seen shortly after leaving Fairbourne on a September day in 1966. There is a very stiff climb towards Friog at this point and No.75009 seems to be making a very energetic assault on the bank. The row of buildings in the middle background is that which lines Fairbourne's main street while the Mawddach estuary is visible beyond them. In the distance lies Barmouth with the mountains of Snowdonia beyond – could one wish for a more captivating panorama? *John Spencer Gilks*

In early 1960 BR decided to change the name of Barmouth Junction station to Morfa Mawddach, the alteration being officially implemented from the start of the summer timetable which came into force on 13th June. Unfortunately, while the public timetables used the revised name, news of the name change had not filtered down to staff on the ground and the station nameboards continued to display the old name for some weeks after 13th June with the result that there was endless confusion among passengers, many of whom were holiday-makers not familiar with the area. One wonders if many were over-carried to Barmouth! Here, 4300 Class 2-6-0 No.7313 poses beside the old nameboard with the 6.55am Wrexham General to Barmouth train on 29th July 1959. *Edwin Wilmshurst*

The signalman at Morfa Mawddach appears to have an armful of single line tokens available to offer to the fireman of BR Standard Class 4MT No.75023 as it takes the sharp curve into the station with a Dolgelly line train in June 1964. Let us hope he gave him the correct one! Before the viaduct across the Mawddach estuary was brought into use passengers travelling to Barmouth were advised to go to Dolgelly and continue their journey by road. The only alternative (according to an 1866 guide) was to use a small boat to reach Barmouth which, as previously mentioned, depending upon the state of the tide, sometimes involved a walk with luggage across a rough, pebbly beach. The guide warned that this was 'a mode of proceeding not very convenient for ladies and children'. *J.W.T. House / Colin Caddy collection*

The end of a perfect day? Photographed from the third coach of the train, an unidentified Collett-designed 2251 Class 0-6-0 approaches Barmouth Junction on (what appears to be) a really lovely evening with the setting sun highlighting the signal box and the station building. The station here is in a picturesque setting and beyond it lie the partly wooded foothills of Cader Idris (2,927 feet above sea level). This picture was taken on 28th August 1959. *Roy Denison*

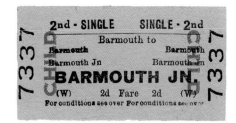

Sunny Barmouth! On what seems to be an absolutely glorious day in June 1963 BR Standard Class 2MT No.78002 approaches Morfa Mawddach station with a two-coach local train probably bound for Dolgelly. In the 1961 summer timetable there were three workings from Barmouth to and from Dolgelly, all of which were advertised as second class only. The train has just crossed Barmouth bridge which carries the Cambrian Coast line across the Mawddach estuary; superb views are obtainable from the train as it traverses the bridge, this being one of the highlights of a journey on the line. *Alan Reeve*

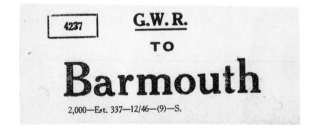

A picture taken at Barmouth on 2nd August 1958 showing 'Dukedog' 4-4-0 No.9018 posing for its picture in the sunshine; the locomotive partially visible on the right is Collett 2251 Class 0-6-0 No.2230. Despite being nominally the oldest locomotive in the class with frames dating back to May 1903, No.9018 survived to become one of the last in traffic. It was one of only five 'Dukedog' 4-4-0s to survive into 1960, these being Nos. 9004/14/15/17/18, and of those, Nos. 9004/15/18 were taken out of service in June which left just two representatives of this very distinctive class. During the peak summer timetable No.9014 was in use on the Ruabon to Barmouth line but No.9017 saw a period of intensive activity during the second week of August when it made a return trip from Machynlleth to Pwllheli on three successive days. On 12th August it piloted No.7818 *Granville Manor* on the up 'Cambrian Coast Express' and worked right through from Machynlleth to Shrewsbury, returning on the corresponding return working. The following day it visited Shrewsbury again, piloting the 9.45am Pwllheli to Paddington train. It seems that No.9017 was the last active member of the class in BR traffic lasting until at least 7th October when it was seen in steam at Machynlleth shed; No.9014 had been put into store at Croes Newydd shed by that date. *P.H. Wells / R.C. Riley collection*

Extract from Western Region winter 1953–54 timetable

Table 189 MACHYNLLETH, TOWYN, BARMOUTH, and PWLLHELI

Miles		Week Days																												Sundays		
		a.m	a.m		a.m	a.m	a.m	a.m	a.m		a.m	p.m		a.m	p.m		p.m	p.m	p.m	p.m	p.m	p.m		p.m	p.m	p.m	p.m	p.m		a.m		
—	Machynlleth .... dep	..	..	..	..	6 50	..	8 5	..	..	..	..	..	1045	..	..	..	1 16	..	..	3 30	..	..	..	5 30	..	6 55	..	..	9 0	..	..
3¾	Dovey Junction ..... arr	..	..	..	..	..	..	8 12	..	..	..	..	..	11 0	..	..	..	1 23	..	..	3 37	..	..	..	5 38	..	7 2	..	..	..	..	..
—	184 Aberystwyth ..... dep	..	..	..	..	..	..	7 30	..	..	..	..	..	9 55	..	..	..	1250	..	..	2 30	..	..	..	4 40	..	6 0	..	..	..	..	..
—	Dovey Junction .... dep	..	..	..	..	..	..	8 15	..	..	..	..	..	1110	..	..	..	1 35	..	..	3 38	..	..	..	5 40	..	7 5	..	..	..	..	..
5½	Gogarth Halt	..	..	..	..	..	..	8 19	..	..	..	..	..	1114	..	..	..	1 39	..	..	Uu	..	..	..	..	..	7 11	..	..	..	..	..
7	Abertafol Halt	..	..	..	..	..	..	8 25	..	..	..		..	1120	..	..	..	1 45	..	..	3 47	..	..	..	5 48	..	Uu	..	..	..	..	..
9	Penhelig Halt	..	..	..	..	7 11	..	8 30	..	..	..		..	1125	..	..	..	1 50	..	..	3 52	..	..	..	5 54	..	7 19	..	..	9 19	..	..
9¾	Aberdovey	..	..	..	..	7 15	..	8 33	..	..	..		..	1129	..	..	..	1 53	..	..	3 56	..	..	..	5 58	..	7 24	..	..	9 23	..	..
13½	Towyn	..	..	..	..	7 27	..	8 47	..	..	..	TC from Liverpool (Lime St.) dep. 7E50, 7S42 a.m. From Bangor dep. 11E30, 11S35 a.m.	..	1138	..	..	..	2 0	..	..	4 6	..	..	—	6 9	..	7 32	..	..	9 31	..	..
15¾	Tonfanau	..	..	..	..	7 33	..	8 54	..	..	..		..	1145	..	..	..	2 6	..	..	4 11	..	..	..	6 14	..	7 38	..	..	9 36	..	..
18	Llangelynin Halt	..	..	..	..	..	..	8 58	..	..	..		..	1149	..	..	..	2 10	..	..	4 15	..	..	..	6 18	..	7 43	..	..	..	..	..
20	Llwyngwril	..	..	..	..	7 41	..	9 3	..	..	..		..	1156	..	..	..	2 20	..	..	4 19	..	..	..	6 22	..	7 49	..	..	9 44	..	..
22¾	Fairbourne	..	..	..	..	7 48	..	9 10	..	..	..		..	12 5	..	..	..	2 27	..	..	4 26	..	..	..	6 30	..	7 57	..	..	9 52	..	..
23¾	Barmouth Junction. arr	..	..	..	..	7 51	..	9 13	..	..	..		..	12 8	..	..	..	2 29	..	..	4 30	..	..	..	6 32	..	8 0	..	..	9 55	..	..
33	187 Dolgelley .... arr	..	..	..	..	..	Ⓐ	9N46	..	..	..		..	1 36	..	..	Ⓐ	3 2	..	..	6Y12	..	..	..	7 41	Ⓐ	9§38	..	..	..	..	..
	dep	..	..	..	..	..	8 30	..	9 30	..	1138		..	..	..	..	1 45	..	..	..	..	4 2	..	5 20	5 20	6 18	..	8 55	..	..	..	..
—	Barmouth Junction. dep	..	..	..	..	7 52	8 52	9 14	10 0	..	12 3		..	1210	..	..	2 7	2 30	..	..	4 31	4 25	..	5 40	6 33	6 40	8 2	9 18	..	9 56	..	..
25½	Barmouth ...... arr	..	..	..	..	7 57	8 57	9 19	10 5	..	12 8		..	1215	..	..	2 12	2 36	..	..	4 36	4 30	..	5 45	6 38	6 45	8 7	9 23	..	10 1	..	..
	dep	..	..	..	..	8 10	..	9 23	..	..	—		..	..	1220	..	..	2 40	..	3 45	..	4 40	..	5 55	6 50	..	8 12	..	..	..	..	..
27	Llanaber Halt	..	..	..	..	..	..	9 26	..	..	..		..	..	1227	..	..	..	..	3 49	..	4 44	..	..	6 54	..	8 16	..	..	..	..	..
29¼	Talybont Halt	..	..	..	..	..	..	9 30	..	..	..		..	..	1232	..	—	..	..	3 53	..	4 48	..	..	6 58	..	8 21	..	..	..	..	..
30½	Dyffryn-Ardudwy	..	..	..	..	8 18	..	9 33	..	..	..		..	..	1236	..	..	2 51		3 57	..	4 51	..	6 4	7 2	..	8 29	..	..	..	..	..
32¾	Talwrn Bach Halt	..		..	..	8 24	..	9 38	..	..	..		..	..	1241	..	..	..		4 2	..	4 56	..	..	7 7	..	8 34	..	..	..	..	..
33½	Llanbedr and Pensarn ..	..		..	..	8 30	..	9 40	..	..	..		..	..	1243	..	..	2 59		4 6	..	5 1	..	6 11	7 10	..	8 37	..	..	..	..	..
34	Llandanwg Halt	..		..	..	8 32	..	9 43	..	..	..		..	..	1247	..	..	..		4 8	..	5 5	..	..	..	..	8 39	..	..	..	..	..
36	Harlech	..	From Bangor dep. 5 30 a.m.	..	..	8 41	..	9 51	..	..	..		..	..	1254	..	..	3 7	From Bangor dep. 2 52 p.m.	4 14	..	5 10	..	6 25	7 18	..	8 46	..	..	..	..	..
38½	Tygwyn Halt	..		..	..	8 46	..	9 55	..	..	..		..	..	1259	..	..	..		4 18	..	5 14	..	..	..	..	8 51	..	..	..	..	..
39½	Talsarnau	..		..	..	8 49	..	9 58	..	..	..		..	..	1 2	..	..	3 13		4 21	..	5 17	..	..	7 24	..	8 54	..	..	..	..	..
40¾	Llandecwyn Halt	..		..	..	8 53	..	10 2	..	..	..		..	..	1 5	..	..	..		4 25	..	5 22	..	..	..	..	8 58	..	..	..	..	..
41½	Penrhyndeudraeth	..		..	..	8 58	..	10 6	..	..	..		..	..	1 8	..	..	3 18		4 31	..	5 26	..	6 36	7 30	..	9 2	..	..	..	..	..
42½	Minffordd	..		..	..	9 2	..	1010	..	..	..		..	..	1 12	..	..	3 23		4 35	..	5 30	..	..	7 34	..	9 6	..	..	..	..	..
44¾	Portmadoc ...... arr	..		..	..	9 6	..	1014	..	..	..		..	..	1 16	..	..	3 27		4 40	..	5 34	..	6 42	7 39	..	9 11	..	..	..	..	..
	dep	6 0		..	..	9 8	..	1017	..	..	..		..	..	1 18	..	..	3 30		4 44	..	5 36	..	6 43	8 15	..	9 14	..	..	..	..	..
48½	Black Rock Halt	..		..	7 40	..	..	1024	..	..	..		..	..	1 25	..	..	..		4 51	..	..	..	..	..	..	..	..	..	..	..	..
49¾	Criccieth	6 12		..	7 51	9 18	..	1030	..	..	..		..	..	1 30	..	..	3 38		4 56	..	5 44	..	6 52	8 24	..	9 22	..	..	..	..	..
53	Afon Wen ...... arr	6 18	..	..	7 57	9 24	..	1036	..	..	..		..	..	1 36	..	..	3 44		5 3	..	5 51	..	6 57	8 30	..	9 28	..	..	..	..	..
	dep	6 25	7 9	..	8 5	9 25	..	1040	..	..	..	1255	..	..	1 49	..	..	3 50	4 19	5 5	..	5 53	..	6 59	8 33	..	9 29	..	..	..	..	..
54½	Penychain D	6 28	7 12	..	8 8	9 28	..	1044	..	..	..	1258	..	..	1 52	..	..	3 54	4 22	5 8	..	5 56	..	7 2	8 36	..	9 32	..	..	..	..	..
55¾	Abererch	..	7 15	..	8 11	9 32	..	1047	..	..	..	1 1	..	..	1 55	..	..	3 58	4 25	5 11	..	5 59	..	7 5	8 39	..	..	..	..	..	..	..
57¾	Pwllheli .... arr	6 35	7 21	..	8 17	9 38	..	1053	..	..	..	1 7	..	..	2 1	..	..	4 5	4 31	5 17	..	6 5	..	7 11	8 45	..	9 40	..	..	..	..	..

D For Pwllheli Holiday Camp
E Except Saturdays
N Third class only
S Saturdays only

TC Through Carriages
Uu Calls to set down passengers on notice being given by the passenger to the Guard at Dovey Junc.

Y First and Third class except Saturdays. Third class only on Saturdays

§ Third class only; arr. 10 6 p.m. on Saturdays
Ⓐ Third class only

OTHER TRAINS between Machynlleth and Dovey Junction, see Table 184—Barmouth Junction and Barmouth, Table 187

Table 189—*continued* PWLLHELI, BARMOUTH, TOWYN, and MACHYNLLETH

Miles		Week Days																													Suns.	
		a.m	a.m	a.m	a.m	a.m	a.m	a.m	a m	a.m	p.m.	p.m	p.m	p.m	p.m	p.m	p.m	p.m	p.m	pm	p.m	p.m	p.m	pm	p.m	p.m	p.m	p.m	p.m	p.m	p.m	p.m	
—	Pwllheli .... dep	5 35	..	6 0	..	7 40	..	..	..	1025	..	..	..	1245	1 35	2 0	..	3 30	3 45	..	..	4 55	5 25	..	..	6 40	..	6 40	..	8 15	..	..	..
2	Abererch	..	..	..	..	7 45	..	..	..	1030	..	..	..	1251	1 40	2 5	..	3 35	3 50	..	..	5 0	5 30	..	..	6 45	..	6 45	..	8 21	..	..	..
3½	Penychain D	..	..	6 7	..	7 48	..	..	..	1034	..	..	..	1255	1 44	2 9	..	3 38	3 53	..	..	5 4	5 33	..	..	6 48	..	6 48	..	8 24	..	..	..
4¾	Afon Wen .... arr	5 45	..	6 11	..	7 52	..	..	..	1037	..	..	..	1258	1 47	2 12	..	3 42	3 57	..	..	5 7	5 36	..	..	6 51	..	6 51	..	8 27	..	..	..
	dep	5 46	..	6 25	..	7 57	..	..	..	1041	..	..	..	1259	1 50		..		4 0	425	..		5 38	..	..	6 58	..	6 58	..	8 34	..	..	..
8	Criccieth	5 52	..	6 32	..	8 3	..	..	..	1047	..	..	..	1 5	1 56		..		4 7	431	..		5 45	..	..	7 4	..	7 4	..	8 40	..	..	..
9½	Black Rock Halt	..	..	..	..	..	..	..	..	1050	..	..	..	1 9	Nn	To Bangor arr 3 39 p.m.	..	To Llandudno Junction arr. 6 16 p.m.	4 10	434	..	To Bangor arr. 6 45 p.m.	5 49	..	..	7 7	..	7 7	..	..	..	..	..
13	Portmadoc ...... arr	6 0	..	6 40	..	8 12	..	..	..	1059	..	..	..	1 16	2 4		..		4 17	442	..		5 55	..	..	7 15	..	7 15	..	8 48	..	..	..
	dep	6 2	..	6 55	..	8 14	..	..	..	11 0	..	..	..	1 17	..		..		4 20	..	..		5 57	..	..	7 40	..	8 15	..	..	..	..	..
15½	Minffordd	6 7	..	7 0	..	8 19	..	..	..	11 5	..	..	..	1 22	..		..		4 25	..	..		6 1	..	..	7 45	..	8 20	..	..	..	..	..
16½	Penrhyndeudraeth	6 11	..	7 4	..	8 23	..	..	..	1112	..	..	..	1 27	..		..		4 32	..	..		6 8	..	..	7 50	..	8 25	..	..	..	..	..
17	Llandecwyn Halt	..	..	7 7	..	8 26	..	..	..	1115	..	..	..	1 30	..		..		4 35	..	..		6 11	..	..	7 55	..	8 28	..	..	..	..	..
18½	Talsarnau	6 16	..	7 12	..	8 31	..	..	..	1120	..	..	..	1 35	..		..		4 40	..	..		6 16	..	..	8 0	..	8 33	..	..	..	..	..
19½	Tygwyn Halt	..	..	7 15	..	8 34	..	..	..	1123	..	..	..	1 38	..		..		4 43	..	..		6 19	..	..	8 3	..	8 36	..	..		..	..
21¾	Harlech	6 23	..	7 20		8 42	..	..	..	1129	..	..	..	1 44	..		..		4 49	..	..		6 24	..	..	8 10	..	8 45	..	..	Saturdays only	..	..
23¾	Llandanwg Halt	..	..	7 25	Except Saturdays	8 47	..	..	..	1134	..	..	..	1 49	..	..	..		4 54	..	..		..	..	..	8 15	..	8 50	..	..		..	..
24¼	Llanbedr and Pensarn ..	6 30	..	7 28		8 50	..	..	..	1138	..	..	..	1 52	..	..	..		4 57	..	..		6 31	..	..	8 20	..	8 54	..	..		..	..
25	Talwrn Bach Halt	6 32	..	7 30		8 52	..	..	..	1140	..	..	..	1 54	..	..	..		5 0	..	..	..	6 33	..	..	8 22	..	8 56	..	..		..	..
27¼	Dyffryn-Ardudwy	6 36	..	7 36		9 2	..	..	..	1146	..	..	..	2 0	..	..	..		5 6	..	..	..	6 39	..	..	8 28	..	9 2	..	..		..	..
28¼	Talybont Halt	6 40	..	7 40		9 6	..	..	..	1150	..	..	..	2 4	..	..	..		5 10	..	..	..	6 43	..	..	8 32	..	9 6	..	..		..	..
30¾	Llanaber Halt	..	..	7 44		9 10	..	..	..	1154	..	..	..	2 8	..	..	..		5 15	..	..	..	..	..	..	8 36	..	9 10	..	..		..	..
32½	Barmouth .... arr	6 47	..	7 48		9 14	Ⓐ	..	..	1158	..	..	..	2 12	..	..	..	..	5 19	..	..	..	6 50	..	..	8 40	Ⓐ	9 14	..	..	Ⓐ	..	..
	dep	6 50	718	..	8 15	..	9 20	9 30	1020	..	12 20	1 10	2 0	2 35	..	..	3 30	..	5 22	..	5Y46	..	..	715	7 30	..	9 10	..	9 25	..	9 40	5 40	..
34	Barmouth Junction. arr	6 55	723	..	8 19	..	9 25	9 35	1025	..	12 25	1 15	2 5	2 40	..	..	3 35	..	5 37	..	5Y51	..	..	720	7 35	..	9 15	..	9 30	..	9 45	5 45	..
43½	187 Dolgelley .... arr	..	743	..	..	..	9 46	..	1046	..	..	1 36	..	3 2	..	..	..	..	..	..	6Y12	..	..	741	..	..	9 38	..	..	..	10 6	..	..
	dep	..	..	..	..	..	..	8N30	..	..	11a28	..	1N45	..	..	..	..	..	5 20	..	..	..	..	..	6N18	..	..	..	8 55	..	..	..	..
—	Barmouth Junction..dep	6 57	..	..	8 20	..	..	9 36	..	..	12 27	..	2 8	..	..	..	3 36	..	5 41	..	..	..	..	..	7 36	Except Saturdays	Except Saturdays	Saturdays only	9 32	..	..	5 46	..
35	Fairbourne	7 0	..	..	8 23	..	..	9 40	..	..	12 31	..	2 11	..	..	..	3 39	..	5 45	..	..	..	..	..	7 39				9 36	..	..	5 49	..
37¾	Llwyngwril	7 9	..	..	8 32	..	..	9 49	..	..	12 38	..	2 21	..	..	..	3 47	..	5 55	..	..	..	..	..	7 50				9 45	..	..	5 57	..
39½	Llangelynin Halt	7 13	..	..	8 36	..	..	9 53	..	..	12 42	..	2 25	..	..	..	3 52	..	Nn	..	..	..	..	..	..				9 50	..	..	..	..
42	Tonfanau	7 20	..	..	8 41	..	..	9 59	..	..	12 47	..	2 31	..	..	..	3 57	..	6 4	..	..	..	..	..	7 58				9 55	..	..	6 5	..
44¼	Towyn	7 28	..	..	8 47	..	..	10 5	..	..	12 55	..	2 37	..	..	..	4 8	..	6 10	..	..	..	..	..	8 3				10 0	..	..	6 11	..
48	Aberdovey	7 35	..	..	..	..	..	1011	..	..	1 3	..	2 46	..	..	..	4 15	..	6 17	..	..	..	..	..	8 10				10 7	..	..	6 18	..
48¾	Penhelig Halt	7 38	..	..	..	..	..	1015	..	..	1 6	..	2 49	..	..	..	4 18	..	6 20	..	..	..	..	..	8 13				1011	..	..	6 21	..
50¾	Abertafol Halt	7 43	..	..	..	..	..	1020	..	..	1 11	..	2 54	..	..	..	4 22	..	Nn	..	..	..	..	..	8 19	..	..	..	..	..	..	..	..
52½	Gogarth Halt	Nn	..	..	..	..	..	1026	..	..	1 17	..	3 0	..	..	..	4 29	..	Nn	..	..	..	..	..	8 25	..	..	..	..	..	..	..	..
54	Dovey Junction ..... arr	7 52	..	..	..	..	..	1030	..	..	1 22	..	3 4	..	..	..	4 33	..	6 34	..	..	..	..	..	Nn	..	..	..	..	..	..	..	..
78½	184 Aberystwyth ... arr	8 50	..	..	..	..	..	1145	..	..	2 11	..	..	..	..	..	5S32		7 25	..	..	..	..	..	9 42		..	..	..	..	..	..	..
—	Dovey Junction ..... dep	8 13	..	..	..	..	..	1036	..	..	1 28	..	3 12	..	..	..	4 34	..	6 44	..	..	..	..	..	..	..	..	..	..	..	..	..	..
57¾	Machynlleth .... arr	8 20	..	..	..	..	..	1042	..	..	1 34	..	3 18	..	..	..	4 41	..	6 51	..	..	..	..	..	8 38	..	..	..	1032	..	..	6 41	..

a a.m.
D For Pwllheli Holiday Camp

E Except Saturdays
N Third class only

Nn Calls to set down passengers on notice being given by the passenger to the Guard at previous *stopping* station

S Saturdays only
Y First and Third class except Saturdays. Third class only on Saturdays
Ⓐ Third class only

OTHER TRAINS between Barmouth and Barmouth Junction, see Table 187—Dovey Junction and Machynlleth, Table 184

Many pictures of trains passing Harlech with the castle as a backdrop have been published over the years but here, for a change, is a picture taken from Harlech castle looking down on the station. This scene was recorded in the summer of 1963 when – judging by the presence of wagons in the yard – Harlech still retained goods facilities. Note the signal box and level crossing in the bottom left hand corner of the photograph. The up platform dates from the 1920s when the GWR undertook a series of improvements to stations in the area. Harlech has always been known as a small intermediate station on the Cambrian coast line but if the North Wales Railway (NWR) had had its way Harlech would also have been an intermediate point on a proposed Shrewsbury–Dolgelly–Porth Dinllaen line. This proposal actually got as far as receiving the Royal Assent, on 21st July 1845, but later the deputy chairman was found to have made a secret loan to another railway and scrutiny of the NWR's books revealed wholesale irregularities. The scandal sunk the NWR without trace and it was never heard of again. *Stuart Ackley collection*

On 26th April 1958 the Festiniog Railway Society sponsored a special train, presumably in connection with their annual general meeting at Portmadoc. The train was powered as far as Ruabon by the record breaking GWR 4-4-0 No.3440 *City of Truro,* but there two 'Dukedogs' took over for the rest of the run through the glorious Welsh countryside to Minffordd, where the station provides direct access to the Festiniog Railway's narrow gauge station. In this photograph the two beautifully prepared 'Dukedogs', Nos. 9017 and 9014, are seen glinting in the sunshine at Minffordd after arrival with the rail tour. The former locomotive was withdrawn in October 1960, by which time it had become the last survivor of its class, and went into store at Oswestry works while enthusiasts raised sufficient money to ensure its preservation. Sixteen months later No.9017 was purchased – one of the first examples of a locomotive being saved by voluntary effort – and made the long trek under its own steam down to the Bluebell Railway in East Sussex. On arrival on the Southern Region the 'Dukedog' was facing southwards – the Bluebell authorities wanted it facing north – so it made an unscheduled trip down to Brighton for turning purposes, the one and only time an engine of this class has visited the south coast. *Derek Penney*

The Collett 2251 Class 0-6-0s were a common sight on the Cambrian lines for many years but 1964 proved to be their final full year of service on the routes around Machynlleth. The station nameboard immediately identifies the location of this picture, the locomotive being No.3208, and this portrait was taken on 13th July 1964. This locomotive survived to become one of the last three active members of its class on the Cambrian section, based at Machynlleth shed, the others being Nos. 2236 and 2268. In late 1964 No.3208 was still in regular use on trains between Dovey Junction and Pwllheli but, amazingly, was moved to Llandudno Junction (presumably via the Afon Wen to Caernarvon line which was still open) for use as the snowplough locomotive and reportedly made at least three trips to Trawsfynydd in this capacity, despite still being officially allocated to Machynlleth. The last Collett 0-6-0 to be used on the Cambrian lines was apparently No.2236 on 25th May 1965, and thus ended a very long association with the area. *Colin Caddy*

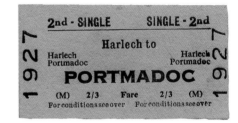

The western extremities of the Cambrian Coast line do not seem to have been widely photographed in colour, perhaps because in steam days many enthusiasts travelled only as far as Minffordd or Portmadoc with a visit to the Festiniog Railway in mind. This is the eastern end of the exceptionally neat and tidy station at Criccieth with the signal box on the left and main station building on the right. Note the very attractive canopy at the front of the station and interesting selection of chimney pots on the station building. This picture is thought to have been taken in the early 1960s. *Stuart Ackley collection*

The western end of Criccieth station with BR Standard Class 3MT 2-6-2T No.82020 pausing with a train bound for Pwllheli in June 1964. No.82020 was built at Swindon and out-shopped in September 1954; it was the first of the second series of these locomotives to be constructed at the works. This machine worked from Nuneaton shed for a time early in its career and was later based at Wrexham (Rhosddu) depot prior to moving to Machynlleth; it was withdrawn from service in September 1965. *J.W.T. House / Colin Caddy collection*

Pwllheli station – journey's end. Actually, in this case it is journey's beginning because the train seen here is awaiting departure. The locomotive is BR Standard Class 3MT No.82020 which is depicted in the previous shot taken on the same day – presumably the photographer simply caught the train from Criccieth. Perhaps surprisingly for a modest terminus, Pwllheli had an engine shed and, even more surprisingly, it was the third of three sheds built to serve the line. The first shed was erected in 1867 and stood until 1927 (the year the new station opened) after which locomotives were berthed in the former carriage shed, an extraordinarily long, wooden building but, presumably, it fulfilled the purpose. It is thought that the former carriage shed dated back to the opening of the line in the late 1860s so it had really stood the test of time. This was replaced in 1958 with a new depot which is understood to be the last shed designed for steam traction to be built by the WR; it was closed after a brief career in railway use in 1966. *J.W.T. House / Colin Caddy collection*

CAMBRIAN COAST LINE

The Moat Lane Junction to Brecon line was constructed by two separate companies, the Moat Lane to Llanidloes stretch was originally part of the Llanidloes & Newtown Railway and opened on 31st August 1859; this local concern was one of four companies which formed the Cambrian Railways in July 1864. The line southwards from Llanidloes to Brecon was built by the Mid Wales Railway, the first sod being cut during torrential rain near Rhayader on 2nd September 1859. South of Llanidloes the route taken by the line was really attractive; initially the line followed the course of the Afon Dulas, reaching the summit of 947 feet above sea level at Pantydwr and this eventually became the highest point on the Cambrian Railways' system. Then the line traversed the Marteg valley, through Marteg tunnel, and along a narrow gorge to emerge into the Wye Valley before reaching Rhayader. A notable engineering work south of Builth Wells was a lattice girder bridge over the river Wye near Boughrood. The formal opening took place on 23rd August 1864 when a special train ran from Brecon to Llanidloes while ordinary passenger services, which comprised three passenger workings and two mixed trains, commenced on 21st September. Three Cambrian Railways trains ran between Llanidloes and Moat Lane Junction where they connected with services on the main line. The last-mentioned station was latterly the northern limit of operations (apart from a few services that went to Newtown) and trains to and from Brecon had their own platform at Moat Lane Junction, this being dead straight unlike the later main line platforms on the other side of the station building which were on a curve. This picture shows the Mid Wales platform at Moat Lane Junction in the early 1960s. Locomotives working services to and from Brecon were housed in an engine shed (not visible in the picture) which was a sub-shed of Oswestry. *Stuart Ackley collection*

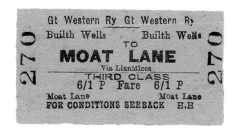

A feature of operations on the Moat Lane Junction to Brecon line was the number of short workings and in the summer 1961 timetable most of these ran between Moat Lane and Llanidloes plus one or two between Builth Road and Three Cocks Junction or Brecon. One of these short workings in seen in this photograph which was taken at Llanidloes on 4th August 1962; the train in view is the 8.05am to Moat Lane Junction with tender-first Ivatt Class 2MT 2-6-0 No.46511 in charge. The engine shed at Llanidloes, located north of the station, was a two-road affair with brick walls and a slate roof and its history could be traced back to the opening of the line in 1859; it was latterly a sub-shed of Oswestry. In 1947 it is recorded that the shed had an allocation of four 0-6-0 tender locomotives. The closure of the line in December 1962 must have been a huge blow to the local community because forty BR members of staff were made redundant at Llanidloes. *Edwin Wilmshurst*

The imposing and rather ornate station building at Llanidloes, seen here in this early 1960s view, was originally the headquarters of the Llanidloes & Newtown Railway and, mercifully, it has survived as a tangible reminder of the railway age in the town. Note that the side wall of the main building, and also that of the gentlemen's toilet, have been tile-hung to keep out the prevailing wind and rain. An interesting feature of the line between Llanidloes and the next station, Tylwch, was the site of Pentpontbren Junction where the course of the ill-fated Manchester & Milford Railway's route could be seen. This was planned to cross the mountains in order to reach Pencader but in the event only the short section as far as Llangurig was constructed and no scheduled train ever ran over this stretch of line. *Stuart Ackley collection*

Extract from Western Region winter 1953–54 timetable

The Moat Lane Junction to Brecon line was arguably one of the most appealing rural lines in Wales offering an unhurried journey through a largely unspoilt landscape of fast flowing rivers, rolling hills and picturesque towns and villages. One of the most scenic sections was between Tylwch and Rhayader and this picture was taken by a photographer who was travelling on the 9.55am from Moat Lane to Brecon on 22nd August 1959 which appears to have been a lovely summer's day. This shot gives a hint of what a journey on this delightful line was like, slowly jogging along behind an Ivatt Class 2MT 2-6-0 past some of the most glorious scenery imaginable. For the record the locomotive on this occasion was No.46522 of Oswestry shed. *John Langford*

A shot that conveys the irresistible charm and breathtaking scenic splendours of the Mid Wales line. Sheep graze in the foreground as an unidentified Ivatt Class 2MT 2-6-0 passes by on a train bound for Moat Lane Junction. This picture was taken near Tylwch Halt, 3¼ miles south of Llanidloes, on 23rd April 1962. *Gerald Daniels*

During the Beeching era in the 1960s BR's detractors often accused it of undertaking unnecessary civil engineering work on lines under threat in order to strengthen the case for closure. After all, a costly replacement bridge here, or a brand new length of track there, could tip the balance in favour of closing a line which would no doubt delight government officials at the Department of Transport many of whom had, apparently, already written the railways out of their plans for the future. When this picture of Ivatt Class 2MT 2-6-0 No.46508 working a southbound civil engineer's train was taken at Rhayader on 13th September 1962 the fate of this lovely line was probably already known but, even so, one is tempted to query the purpose of this train. Perhaps BR planned to relay a set of points in a disused goods yard somewhere down the line – or is that just being cynical? Rhayader station was situated on the western fringe of the town and, indeed, there are no buildings visible in this shot, only a few animals grazing in the field on the left. Rhayader was located at the end of the seven miles-long descent from the watershed of the line at Pantydwr. The station buildings, goods shed and base of the water tank were very solidly built of stone, which was presumably quarried locally. The platform facings were also of stone but passengers alighting at Rhayader had to have their wits about them because the platforms were very low and no doubt presented quite a challenge to elderly people. The goods yard consisted of five roads, three of which were loops which made life easier for the operating staff. *Graham Mallinson*

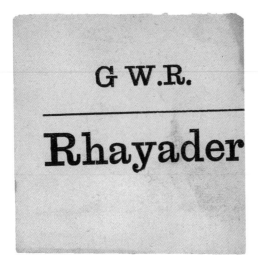

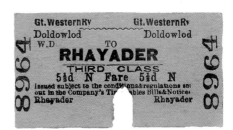

Builth Road (Low Level) is one of the most easily recognised stations on the Moat Lane Junction to Brecon line because this is the point where the Central Wales Line passes overhead on the bridge which is clearly visible in the background. There was a walkway and luggage lift (visible on the right) between the two stations and at one time there was also a curve connecting the routes, but this was only used for goods purposes, apart from being traversed by the Royal train in 1904. Originally the station consisted of one platform which boasted only a simple timber waiting shelter but in 1893 another platform was added for up trains together with a passing loop and more substantial buildings were built on the down platform. In this picture the two-coach 9.10am to Three Cocks Junction poses in the sunshine with Ivatt 2-6-0 No.46523 in charge on 14th April 1962. *John Langford*

A closer view of the lift at Builth Road that facilitated the transfer of luggage and parcels between the two stations. One wonders how many country stations had such a relatively sophisticated piece of equipment and who repaired it when it broke down! The low level tracks are in the foreground while the high level station is partially visible; note the signs that left passengers intending to catch Central Wales line trains in no doubt regarding which platform they had to use. *Stuart Ackley collection*

In some respects Builth Wells station had the best service of any on the Moat Lane Junction to Brecon line because in the early 1960s trains were provided to and from Builth Road (Low Level) solely to connect with the 9.07am and 7.50pm departures from the High Level station to Swansea, thus avoiding the painfully slow journey to South Wales via Brecon (note the times quoted refer only to the summer 1961 timetable). In this illustration Ivatt Class 2MT 2-6-0 No.46523 waits at Builth Wells with the 9.10am from Builth Road to Three Cocks Junction on 14th April 1962. The photographer comments that this train was allowed no less than 17 minutes at Builth Wells, this wait being extremely convenient for any visiting railway photographers! Note the vintage gentlemen's toilet on the right and barrow loaded with parcels on the opposite platform. There may have been substantial parcels traffic at Builth Wells but it is unlikely that passenger business was brisk due to the station's location on the opposite bank of the river Wye to the town centre. Remarkable though it may seem, the Cambrian Railways constructed a small engine shed at Builth Wells in 1864 and latterly this had low buttressed brick walls with corrugated upper walls and roof; this establishment lasted until September 1957. *John Langford*

Unfortunately, some of the stations on the Moat Lane Junction to Brecon line were distant from the settlements they purported to serve, a not uncommon situation on many rural lines! Erwood station was about a mile away from the hamlet of the same name and, in any case, Erwood was on the main road that ran southwards from Builth Wells towards Brecon so railway passengers are unlikely to have been numerous. Trains regularly crossed there and in this illustration, thought to date from the early 1960s, a tender-first Ivatt Class 2MT 2-6-0, hauling a northbound train, waits in the loop as sister engine No.46511 arrives with a train bound for Brecon. The signal box is out of sight on the left while not far away runs the river Wye – what a peaceful spot this must have been. *Stuart Ackley collection*

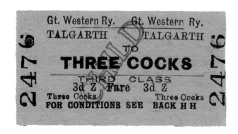

A junction station with the line to Hereford almost in the middle of nowhere. The nearest place of any real consequence to Three Cocks Junction, apart from the adjacent hamlet of Aberllyfni, was Hay-on-Wye, about 5½ miles to the north-east while Brecon was more than 11 miles away. Three Cocks was a typical British country junction station where nothing happened for hours on end and then, all of a sudden, inter-connecting trains arrived from all directions almost simultaneously. The long gaps between trains at least gave the staff time to tidy the station which was neatly maintained with attractive flower beds for passengers to admire. Travellers arriving after the two hours-long marathon journey from Moat Lane Junction were probably feeling a trifle thirsty and no doubt welcomed the golden opportunity to obtain a quick drink in the refreshment room if they had time but, regrettably, some trains paused only briefly at Three Cocks thus denying their passengers the chance. One wonders if the manager of the refreshment room had ever approached BR with a request to space out the trains more evenly so he could avoid a rush of customers at certain times of the day! This shot, looking towards Brecon on the Hereford side of the station, is thought to have been taken in the early 1960s. *Stuart Ackley collection*

The rush hour at Three Cocks. A comprehensive portrait of Three Cocks Junction station and tiny goods yard, showing the track layout and signalling arrangements with the Moat Lane Junction line on the left and Hereford route in the middle of the shot. Note that the roads in the goods yard are actually loop lines, a feature seen at other stations on the Mid Wales line. For the record the trains, and their respective locomotives (from left to right), are the 1.20pm Brecon to Moat Lane Junction with No.46510 in charge which is barely visible, an unidentified Ivatt Class 2MT on the 12.30pm Builth Road (Low Level) to Brecon which has the 'road' and No.46513 on the 2.15pm Three Cocks to Hereford which connected with the two aforementioned trains. After these services departed peace and tranquillity was restored and the refreshment room manager would be able to go for a long nap! *John Langford*

The official name of this station was, of course, Talyllyn Junction, but nameboards on this station were abbreviated for some obscure reason. This sign was located on a platform served only by Mid Wales trains which was separated from the principal part of the station by a boarded crossing. The black and white traditional 'pagoda' waiting shelter does not look too welcoming! *Martin Smith*

Talyllyn Junction, located 7¾ miles from Three Cocks Junction, was where the line from Newport joined the Moat Lane Junction to Brecon line and in this view Ivatt Class 2MT 2-6-0 No.46501 is seen leaving with the 1.20pm Brecon to Moat Lane working on a sunny 6th October 1962. The route from Newport made a triangular junction with that from Three Cocks and Talyllyn Junction station was on the western end. It should be noted that Brecon was the focal point of passenger trains in the area and the eastern curve, that enabled trains to run directly from Three Cocks Junction to Merthyr and Newport, was not heavily used. Talyllyn Junction was the southern limit of the Mid Wales Railway's property, the rest of the line to Brecon being the route of the former Brecon & Merthyr Railway (B&MR). An interesting feature of Talyllyn Junction station was the 674 yards-long tunnel at the western end, this being originally built by the Hay Railway who operated a 24 miles-long horse tramway from Brecon to Aberllyfni (Three Cocks) and on to Eardisley north of the river Wye. The tunnel, said to be the oldest in Great Britain, was opened on 7th May 1816 and enlarged and reopened by the B&MR on 1st May 1863. *Martin Smith*

Photographed on the penultimate day of passenger services to the town of Brecon, the three-coach 12.10pm from Brecon to Newport is seen departing from Talyllyn Junction behind 8750 Class 0-6-0PT No.9616 on 28th December 1962. At this time much of Great Britain was carpeted in snow and the station seen here, which was 610 feet above sea level, had clearly received its fair share. One wonders what was in the thoughts of the enginemen in charge of No.9616 which was leaking steam from every pore. They would have been faced with the daunting prospect of surmounting the notorious Seven Mile Bank from Talybont-on-Usk which involved 6½ miles climbing at 1 in 38 up to the 925 feet contour and this with a locomotive obviously in a parlous condition. In addition, if they were based at Brecon, there would also have been thoughts of looming redundancy. Note the magnificent stone-built signal box on the right. *Hugh Ballantyne*

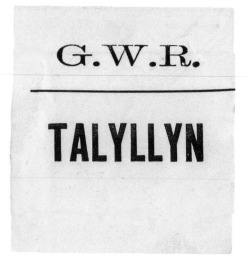

A snowy farewell. Ivatt Class 2MT 2-6-0 No.46515 stands in Brecon station with an unidentified working on 28th December 1962, the penultimate day of passenger operations. All of the routes radiating from Brecon lost their passenger services from 31st December but, because there was no Sunday service, the final day of operation was 29th December. The station building cannot be said to be especially attractive and the premises suffered from a major drawback because there was little protection from the elements, apart from a short, arched canopy in front of the main building so the station, which was located on higher ground than the town below, could be really bleak and uninviting on a bad day. A 50ft turntable, inspection pit and coaling stage were provided behind the bay platform which can be seen on the left beyond the station building. The closure of all the routes radiating from Brecon, totalling 170 route-miles, was one of the most contentious, controversial and bitterly contested proposals made by the government. BR cited annual losses of £290,000 and, not surprisingly, the line to Moat Lane Junction was stated to be the biggest loss-maker of all. Despite the fact that 2,700 journeys were being made daily on the routes involved the closures went ahead without BR making any attempt to improve services or achieve economies, a scenario sadly repeated on many lines up and down Great Britain. The use of steam locomotives right to the end on two- and three-coach trains may have been a real bonus for the enthusiast but the extra costs of steam traction doubtless strengthened the case for closure. *Hugh Ballantyne*

G.W.R.

Brecon

Fleur-de-lis Platform, Darran & Deri and Pentir Rhiw are just three of the intermediate stations on the 47 miles-long Brecon to Newport line, one of the most spectacular routes in Wales. Not all of the 21 stations on the line had such fascinating names but the railway writer and historian D.S.M. Barrie once said that 'every mile of the 47 miles between Brecon and Newport was full of railway interest or scenic splendour'. Largely built by the Brecon & Merthyr Railway (B&MR) this company was the first to serve Brecon with services from Pant, near Dowlais, commencing on 1st May 1863, but the line to Newport did not open throughout until 1868. The engineer for the B&MR, Henry Conybeare, characterised the new railway as 'a good locomotive road throughout' but his assertion conveniently overlooked the fact that after crossing the river Usk at Talybont the line climbed southwards through the Brecon Beacons up the notorious 6½ miles of 1 in 38 gradient known as Seven Mile Bank, rising 925 feet in the process to a summit at Torpantau 1,313 feet above sea level. Talybont-on-Usk station is depicted in this early 1960s shot which shows the substantial stone-built station and water tank; the goods shed, which was used as an engine shed between 1863 and 1900, is hidden by the station buildings. The outstanding scenery surely speaks for itself. *Gerald Daniels*

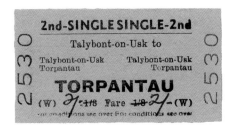

Photographed against the splendid background of a reservoir in the heart of the Brecon Beacons, the 12.10pm train from Brecon to Newport, with 8750 Class 0-6-0PT No.4611 in charge, is pictured at Pentir Rhiw on 14th April 1962. The 47 miles-long journey was one of the longest runs for a pannier tank locomotive and the, no doubt, fairly frequent water stops at least gave the crew and their engine time to catch their breath in between the climbs. Pentir Rhiw station was the halfway point on the long, hard slog up to the summit at the isolated station of Torpantau. One wonders why a station was provided at such a remote spot as Torpantau, there being no habitation in the immediate area apart from one or two farmhouses. Torpantau was, however, a strategic location used regularly to cross trains so, perhaps, that is why a station was constructed at that spot. It is likely the only regular passengers were hikers, there being a fairly direct path down to Brecon. *John Langford*

Pontsticill Junction was an attractive and brightly-painted station where the line from Brecon divided, the main route going to Newport while another descended to Merthyr, 6¾ miles distant, on almost continuous 1 in 45/50 gradients. Passengers to and from Merthyr were clearly not encouraged, however, because only two trains were provided in each direction on weekdays between those points and while (in the 1961 summer timetable) both services from Merthyr enabled good connections to be made for Brecon, there was only one reasonable connection in the opposite direction. Pontsticill Junction station is depicted in this portrait which was taken on 6th October 1962, less than three months before closure. There were certainly plenty of seats to choose from – one is tempted to ask if there was slight over provision. *Martin Smith*

A shot taken on 29th December 1962, the last day of regular services, at snow covered Pant station, just north of Dowlais, showing 8750 Class 0-6-0PT No.4679 taking water while working the very last 8.03am Newport to Brecon train. The fireman appears to have overdone the topping up of his locomotive's tanks and water overflows down the tank side and onto the track – an everyday occurrence in steam days. Note the horizontal water pipe which is fed directly from the tank, an unsophisticated but, no doubt, very effective arrangement. Note also the brazier, signal with a wooden post, delightful old signal box and milepost – could one wish for more railway interest in one photograph? Curiously, the mileage exhibited on the post does not correspond with that in the public timetable but, perhaps, the figure in the timetable was calculated from Newport station whereas that on the milepost indicates the mileage from the branch's main line junction. Pant used to be a junction station, but the service to Dowlais Central was withdrawn from 2nd May 1960, however Brecon to Newport trains continued to stop at Dowlais Top station. *Hugh Ballantyne*

BRECON TO NEWPORT

Enginemen working trains from Newport to Hereford faced two formidable banks, the 1 in 95/106 incline up to Pontypool Road and the even more arduous climb at 1 in 82/95 to a summit at the former Llanvihangel station. Here, a rather bedraggled 'Hall' Class 4-6-0, No.6946 *Heatherden Hall,* plods up the bank from Abergavenny to Llanvihangel with a long goods train in tow on 10th April 1964; 7200 Class 2-8-2T No.7240 provides rear-end assistance. By the date of this picture the glory days of WR steam traction were well and truly over and many locomotives were in a disgraceful state as exemplified here by the filthy condition of No.6946 and, indeed, this machine was put out of its misery when it was withdrawn from traffic two months later. *Martin Smith*

The former station at Llanvihangel marked the summit of the Newport to Hereford line in both directions and must have been an excellent spot to observe traffic in steam days with the sound of hard-pressed locomotives reverberating off the hills. In this picture an express, headed by 'Modified Hall' Class 4-6-0 No.6981 *Marbury Hall,* tops the climb with (what appears to be) the 10.17am Exeter St Davids to Manchester Piccadilly, a dated train that ran on Saturdays only during the peak summer season. Note that this pleasantly situated country station, which was closed from 9th June 1958, had staggered platforms and a dainty signal box. This picture was taken on 18th August 1962. *R.C. Riley*

Gt .Western Ry   Gt. Western Ry
Llanvihangel Mon Llanvihangel Mon
TO
PANDY
THIRD CLASS
4d N Fare 4d N
Issued subject to the conditions & regulations set
out in the Company's Time Tables, Bills & Notices
Pandy   Pandy
052   052

A view of Dolau station, looking northwards, in May 1964 just before the implementation of the principal BR economies on the Central Wales line which involved track rationalisation, the withdrawal of through goods trains and, of course, the elimination of steam traction. Dolau station, which served a tiny hamlet, was located on one of the double track sections that were rapidly reduced to a single line only. Judging by the state of the paintwork on the station building and signal box BR had been economising at Dolau for years and pursuing a deliberate policy of systematic neglect – how could they let the place get into such a terrible state? Even the vintage station nameboard is almost illegible. *Gerald Daniels*

The Central Wales Line was constructed to convey coal to industry in the Midlands and north of England and enable those areas' exports to reach the ports of Swansea and Milford Haven. The line was built in stages by a series of small private companies, the first section from Llanelli to Llandovery opening throughout in 1858 and the latter place became the goal of railway promoters aiming southwards from Shropshire. The next stretch to be brought into use was the 12 miles-long Craven Arms to Knighton section which was opened throughout by the Knighton Railway on 6th March 1861. The 20 miles-long Knighton to Llandrindod Wells stretch, promoted by the Central Wales Railway, took five years to complete owing to financial problems and this opened on a piecemeal basis, with the last section from Penybont to Llandrindod Wells being brought into use on 10th October 1865. One of the highlights of this section of line is the 190 yards-long Knucklas viaduct, a 13-arch stone castellated structure that takes the line across the Heyop valley. The Central Wales Extension Railway obtained an Act on 3rd July 1860 to take the line southwards to Llandovery, a distance of 26¼ miles, and this stretch of the route was also opened in stages as construction progressed, the final section being commissioned on 8th October 1868. This is the most heavily engineered stretch of the line and includes the summit of the route at 820 feet above sea level south of Llanrwtyd Wells. The London & North Western Railway (L&NWR) absorbed all three of these local companies and in 1871 that

company won a legal battle to give it control of the line. Most of the route was built as a double track formation and this was actually laid on some sections, only to be abandoned in the 1960s to reduce expenditure; many passing loops were taken out at the same time. The final steam-hauled passenger train was reportedly the 6.25pm Swansea to York mail hauled by Stanier Class 5MT 4-6-0 No.45406 on 13th June 1964. In the late 1960s BR proposed closure of the line but, mercifully, its social value was recognised and it survived. The L&NWR tradition on the line ensured that it would have a totally different character to other lines in mid-Wales where the GWR was dominant and it is difficult to believe that this picture, which depicts an 8F Class 2-8-0 shunting at Penybont, was actually taken in Wales. The Llanbister Road to Penybont section was doubled in 1871, only to revert to a single line in June 1964 when BR economies started to bite. Note that historical information about the section of line south of Llandovery to Swansea Victoria is provided in a later caption. *John Spencer Gilks*

'Builth Road High Level – Change for Builth Wells, Brecon, Rhayader and Llanidloes' states the station nameboard at Builth Road on 18th March 1961. Note the sign directing passengers to the low level station. A Shrewsbury to Swansea Victoria train is seen standing in the southbound platform with Fowler-designed Class 4MT 2-6-4T No.42388 in charge. A total of 125 of these distinctive locomotives was built at Derby works, the first entering traffic in November 1927; No.42388 was one of a later batch, not appearing until May 1933. At the time of this photograph it was one of about half a dozen of these machines based at Landore shed, Swansea, for use on Central Wales Line services on which they penetrated deep into former GWR territory. *Edwin Wilmshurst*

L. M. & S. R.
Builth Road

THE CENTRAL WALES LINE

Steam in the Welsh landscape – *par excellence*. Photographed against a breathtaking mountain backdrop, a Swansea to Shrewsbury passenger train, hauled by an unidentified BR Standard Class 5MT 4-6-0, climbs towards Sugar Loaf tunnel in July 1963. Is any further comment necessary? *Mike Esau*

The Builth Road to Llandovery stretch is the most heavily engineered section of the Shrewsbury to Swansea line and this includes a long tunnel beneath Sugar Loaf mountain. Another civil engineering feature on this section of the route is this graceful viaduct at Cynghordy which carries the line across the Bran valley. The 100 feet-high viaduct was built on a curve and has a 1 in 60 falling gradient towards Cynghordy station located about a mile away; the viaduct has eighteen brick and sandstone arches. One of the contractor's children was reputed to have been killed during construction of the seventh pier, which is consequently said to be haunted. The glorious scenery though which this line passes is apparent from this photograph, which was taken on 15th May 1964. *Gerald Daniels*

A Shrewsbury to Swansea train, with BR Standard Class 4MT 2-6-4T No.80069 in charge, leaves Pantyffynnon on 15th June 1963. This station was formerly a junction for the 6½ miles-long branch to Brynamman West but this line lost its passenger service from 18th August 1958. This machine was allocated to Swansea (East Dock) shed at the time of this picture. *Roy Patterson / Edwin Wilmshurst collection*

THE CENTRAL WALES LINE

An intriguing photograph showing the 2.40pm Shrewsbury to Swansea (Victoria) train entering Pontardulais Junction on 19th May 1964 shortly before services on this line were turned over to diesel traction and diverted to run to Llanelly. Normally this train would have been powered by a Stanier 'Black Five' or BR Standard Class 4MT 2-6-4T but on this occasion 8750 Class 0-6-0PT No.4676 is in charge and it is reasonable to assume that this engine replaced a much larger failed locomotive further up the line. The train has just branched off the former GWR line from Llandeilo to head south-eastwards on the old L&NWR route towards Swansea (Victoria) which was closed from 15th June 1964. The line northwards from Pontardulais to Llandovery was originally opened in two stages by the Llanelly Railway, the first section as far as Llandeilo being brought into use in 1857 while the final stretch, which was worked on a joint basis with the L&NWR, opened on 1st April 1858. *Hugh Ballantyne*

The Mumbles Road to Swansea (Victoria) section of the Shrewsbury to Swansea route was very different to the dramatic mountain scenery that characterises much of the line because it ran alongside the seashore for the most of the final three miles into Swansea (Victoria) station. In this picture it is difficult to judge where the railway property ends and the beach begins: the prevailing south-westerly wind has blown sand onto the tracks, almost up to rail level. This was one stretch of line where the driver did not have to use the locomotive's sanding equipment, but one wonders how much damage was done to the engine's bearings by sand blowing around on a windy day. In this photograph the 4.15pm Swansea (Victoria) to Pontardulais train, formed of a single coach, is depicted pulling away from Swansea Bay station with 8750 Class 0-6-0PT No.9675 in charge on 15th May 1964, a month before the passenger service was withdrawn. This train was one of half a dozen, purely local weekday workings between those points but the solitary carriage indicates that business was far from brisk and people preferred to use the much more frequent local buses. *Gerald Daniels*

The rather shabby station buildings at Swansea Bay provide a stark contrast to 5600 Class No.5623's gleaming paintwork as it steams into the station with a Pontardulais to Swansea (Victoria) local train on 5th March 1962. The 0-6-2T is really immaculate and presumably it had just been released from Caerphilly works following a general overhaul; the works closed in 1963 but was still undertaking heavy repairs at the time of this picture. The famous Swansea & Mumbles Railway, the history of which can be traced back to 1804, ran parallel to the 'main line' for some distance. In 1959 an Act of Abandonment was obtained and this fascinating line, which at various times had used almost every form of traction imaginable, was closed with effect from 5th January 1960. *Gerald Daniels*

The 1.45pm train from Llandebie, hauled by former GWR pannier tank locomotive No.3777, enters Swansea (Victoria) station on 8th September 1961. This train was the only regular working in the summer 1961 timetable advertised to start from Llandebie. Opened on 14th December 1867 the line from Pontardulais was originally built as a single track route but was later doubled by the L&NWR. The line passed over the GWR's South Wales main line six miles east of Llanelly. The station appears to be rather deserted in this shot which is not surprising as it was served only by Central Wales trains. The summer 1961 timetable lists five trains each way daily between Swansea and Shrewsbury and in addition there were a few short workings; the next scheduled departure after the arrival at 2.40pm of the train seen here would have been the 4.15pm 'local' to Pontardulais. Perhaps the best-known train from Swansea (Victoria) station was the overnight mail to York where it arrived at the ungodly hour of 3.40am. Surprisingly, on Saturdays this working stopped at almost all of the small wayside stations on the Central Wales line so any passenger from, say, Dolau who just happened to be travelling to York probably could not believe their luck provided, of course, that they had somebody willing to pick them up at the other end in the middle of the night. Perhaps the barrow-load of mail waiting on the platform was destined to be Swansea's 'contribution' to the mail train that evening! *Hugh Ballantyne*

On 2nd July 1960 the Stephenson Locomotive Society (Midland Area) sponsored a rail tour which started at Bridgend and visited branch lines in the local valleys; for the principal part of the tour the train was formed of a three-coach auto set with 6400 Class 0-6-0PT No.6416 sandwiched in the middle. After travelling up the line to Blaengarw, which lost its passenger service from 9th February 1953, the train ran up the branch to Nantymoel, part of the former Ogmore Valley Railway line that opened to traffic from Tondu on 1st August 1865. Passenger services, which had latterly comprised half a dozen trains each way on weekdays only, were withdrawn from 5th May 1958 but the branch remained in business for goods traffic. Pictured against a rather sombre backdrop of mountains, the train is seen standing in the dilapidated former Nantymoel station with many of the participants walking across the track – the attitude of the authorities was much more relaxed at that time. Strangely, despite having closed more than two years previously the station retained its rather battered nameboard. *Gerald Daniels*

After the trip up to Nantymoel the train returned to Tondu and continued to Caerau where the enthusiasts temporarily changed onto another train for the journey along the former South Wales Mineral Railway line via Glyncorrwg to North Rhondda Halt. This line was opened from Briton Ferry to Tonmawr tunnel in June 1861 and extended to Glyncorrwg in March 1863 to serve various collieries. Originally broad gauge, it was converted to standard gauge in May 1872 and taken over by the GWR in 1907. A passenger service was run from Cymmer to Glyncorrwg for the benefit of local passengers but only lasted from 28th March 1918 to 22nd September 1930. Here, 8750 Class 0-6-0PT No.9634 is depicted at the former Glyncorrwg station, with its train of three vintage National Coal Board carriages, prior to tackling the ferocious climb up to North Rhondda Halt. Once again, brooding, dark, distant mountains provide an almost intimidating background. *Gerald Daniels*

The trip along the fiercely graded, most northerly section of the line from Glyncorrwg up to North Rhondda Halt was probably the highlight of the day for most participants. This section remained *in situ* primarily to serve the pits in the valley but was also used by miners' trains to and from Glyncorrwg. These workmen's services had previously run from Cymmer, further down the valley, but had been cut back to Glyncorrwg. The run up to North Rhondda Halt must have been a wonderfully exhilarating experience for passengers as pannier tank locomotive No.9634 forged its way up the narrow valley with the deafening sound of its sharp exhaust no doubt echoing back off the hills. Initially the gradient from Glyncorrwg was a relatively trifling 1 in 28 but incredibly this steepened to 1 in 22 – one can only imagine the noise that emanated from No.9634. Here the train is seen at North Rhondda Halt; note the colliery waste tip virtually on top of the mountain. Later the tour covered lines in the Llantrisant and Penygraig areas before terminating at Cardiff (General). What a day! *Gerald Daniels*

One of the most steeply graded lines in South Wales, and indeed in the whole of the principality, was the branch from Nelson & Llancaiach to Dowlais (Cae Harris) which climbed up to the 1,250ft contour on gradients as steep as 1 in 35. The relatively obscure 9½ miles-long, double track Taff Bargoed Railway, built jointly by the GWR and Rhymney Railway, was opened in 1876 principally to transport iron ore to the hungry furnaces at Dowlais which was one of the largest steel making centres in the world at that time. Some of the climbs on the route were quite astonishing, such as the 3½ miles from Nelson & Llancaiach to the intermediate station of Bedlinog (800ft above sea level) during which the line ascended 300ft. It was said that a cold, frosty night was the best time to witness the fleeting sight and incredible sound of two locomotives, one at the front and one pushing at the rear, heaving a heavy iron ore train towards Dowlais and, even at Trelewis, near Nelson, the labouring locomotives could sometimes be heard until they reached the summit at Cwmbargoed, six miles distant. Passenger services on the route latterly consisted of four trains each way on Mondays to Fridays with extra workings on Saturdays; there was no Sunday service. In this picture 5600 Class 0-6-2T No.5626 is seen at Dowlais (Cae Harris) station in June 1963 apparently propelling the empty stock of an earlier arrival out of the station in order to run around its train. Passenger trains were withdrawn from 13th June 1964. *Martin Smith*

Table 139				NELSON AND LLANCAIACH and DOWLAIS												

Week Days only

Miles		W a.m J	a.m		Y p.m S	p.m E	p.m S	p.m Y		Y p.m Y	J p.m S	p.m S			E Except Saturdays
—	Nelson & Llancaiach dep	6 47	9 35	..	1247	3 15	3 20	5 50	..	8 25	1013	1142	..	..	..	**J** To and from Hengoed (H.L.), (Table 137)
1	Trelewis Platform	6 51	9 38	..	1250	3 18	3 23	5 53	..	8 28	1016	1144	..	..	..	
3½	Bedlinog	7 6	9 46	..	1 23	3 31	3 31	6 4	..	8 36	1024	1152	..	..	..	**S** Saturdays only
6½	Cwm Bargoed	7 19	9 58	..	1 15	3 43	3 44	6 18	..	8 49	1035	12 6	..	..	..	**W** Workmen's Train
9½	Dowlais (Cae Harris) arr	7 27	10 7	..	1 23	3 52	3 53	6 26	..	8 57	1044	1215	..	..	..	**Y** To and from Ystrad Mynach (Table 137)

Week Days only

Miles		W a.m Y	a.m J	a.m Z		W p.m E	p.m S	p.m Y		Y p.m Y	J p.m S	p.m S			Z To Ystrad Mynach on Saturdays arr. 12 7 p.m. (Table 137)
—	Dowlais (Cae Harris) dep	5 20	7 38	1132	..	1 15	3 24	4 15	..	6 43	9 15	1055	..	..	..
2½	Cwm Bargoed	5 29	7 47	1141	..	1 25	4 4	4 24	..	6 52	9 24	11 3	..	..	..
6	Bedlinog	5 37	7 55	1149	..	1 35	4 4	4 32	..	7 0	9 32	1111	..	..	..
8½	Trelewis Platform	5 45	8 3	1157	..	1 44	4 54	4 40	..	7 9	9 37	1116	..	..	..
9½	Nelson & Llancaiach arr	5 49	8 6	12 0	..	1 48	4 57	4 43	..	7 11	9 40	1120	..	..	..

Extract from Western Region winter 1953–54 timetable

Pictured against the weird shapes of the Dowlais waste tips, 5600 Class 0-6-2T No.5602 is seen under the coaling stage at Dowlais (Cae Harris) shed on 19th May 1964. The largely stone-built shed, which had a slate roof and timber gables, was situated about 250 yards from the station and also had a 50ft turntable at the rear, but this was rarely used because locomotives usually worked bunker-first from Dowlais. Inexplicably, the coaling stage and water tower were located on the opposite side of the running lines for many years, but in about 1958 a new coaling plant, clad in corrugated steel, was provided at the shed and this is partially visible on the right of the shot towering above the 5600 Class locomotive. The reliable and rugged engines of this class monopolised workings over the line from Nelson for many years. *Hugh Ballantyne*

Class 5600 0-6-2T No.5651 waits patiently at Dowlais (Cae Harris) station also on 19th May 1964 prior to leaving with the 11.32am departure to Ystrad Mynach. The station here consisted of one main platform and a short bay (on the right) which was generally used for storing coaching stock. A single track ran across the High Street into a local steel works. *Hugh Ballantyne*

Almost up in the clouds. Crumlin viaduct, one of the marvels of Victorian railway engineering, carried the 41¾ miles-long Pontypool Road to Neath line 200ft above the Ebbw valley and was opened on 1st June 1857. It was built for the Taff Vale extension of the Newport, Abergavenny & Hereford Railway and is reputed to have cost only £41 7s (£41.35) per foot run, a very low figure even for those days. The viaduct was actually in two separate parts which were divided by a narrow ridge of high ground. The principal portion of the structure, over the Ebbw valley, consisted of seven spans while the shorter section over the Kendon valley had three spans. All of the spans were 150ft long and made of wrought iron and supported on piers made up of fourteen 12inch diameter cast-iron columns braced together. The total length including masonry abutments was 1,658ft, the height from the bottom of the foundations to the top of the handrail being 208ft. Most of the piers rested on solid rock but two were on masonry built up from hard gravel some 14ft below ground level. On 8th December 1853, when the first pier was in position, an inscribed cup containing coins was placed in a recess in the stone by the wife of the railway company's chairman. The iron castings were forged in Scotland and the machining and fitting was undertaken on site, there being more than 880 tons of wrought iron in the girders and bracings. The former, each weighing 25 tons, were lifted into position using ropes and tackle. On 7th May 1857 the viaduct was tested and a maximum central deflection of 1¼ inch was recorded with trains on each track totalling 380 tons. When the viaduct opened on 1st June 1857 cannons were fired on both sides of the valley while the viaduct and trains were decorated for the occasion; 20,000 people are reported to have attended the celebrations. The total cost of the undertaking was £62,000. Single line operation was introduced over the viaduct on 22nd April 1928 and latterly there was an 8mph speed limit plus weight restrictions on locomotives that could be used. Passenger services, which latterly consisted of five through trains each way, were withdrawn from the Pontypool Road to Neath line from 15th June 1964 and, at the time, there was talk of preserving the viaduct as an ancient monument but, sadly, nothing came of this suggestion. Demolition of the structure commenced in 1965 but at least it had one last moment of glory, if that is quite the right word, when it was reportedly used as a backdrop for a film sequence for the thriller *Arabesque* featuring Sophia Loren who spent the best part of a day walking along a cat walk beneath the viaduct. In this portrait of Crumlin viaduct, taken from Crumlin Low Level station, an eastbound passenger train is seen rumbling across on 31st October 1962. *W. Potter / R.C. Riley collection*

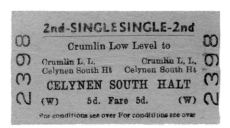

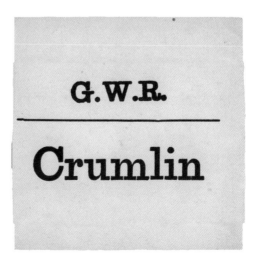

Walnut Tree viaduct, a seven-span lattice steel girder structure constructed by the former Barry Railway, soared 130ft above the river Taff, quadruple track of the Taff Vale Railway and adjacent A470 main road. The 1,500 feet-long structure, which was one of the civil engineering masterpieces of South Wales, enabled the Barry Railway to bridge the Nantgarw gap, south of Taffs Well, a natural defile that marked the limit of the Glamorgan coalfield. Most pictures of this impressive viaduct were taken from high up on the side of the valley but this shot is almost from rail level and gives some idea of its height and scale. Taken on 12th May 1965, it shows bunker-first 5600 Class 0-6-2T No.6614 rumbling across the viaduct with the daily goods train which, by that date, was the last remaining scheduled working. Following closure of the line, the steel girders were removed in 1969 while the massive piers were demolished in 1973. *Hugh Ballantyne*

While Walnut Tree viaduct was certainly a splendid structure, the commanding view obtainable from the top was equally impressive but latterly only enjoyed by a few adventurous enthusiasts. The four-track former Taff Vale Railway dominates the foreground of this picture with the main road cutting across in the middle; the river Taff is out of sight on the left hidden by trees. Taffs Well station is visible beyond the bridge, on the line to Pontypridd, while the route to Caerphilly curves off to the extreme right. 5600 Class No.5692, is seen banking a coal train towards Pontypridd in this picture, which was also taken on 13th May 1965. *Hugh Ballantyne*

THE SOUTH WALES VALLEYS

If asked to name their favourite Welsh route it is unlikely that many railway aficionados would select a little-known line from Llanelly that ran up into the hills above the town as far as Cross Hands. This was a mineral line promoted by the Llanelly & Mynydd Mawr Railway (L&MMR) who obtained an Act in 1875 to convert the remains of the old Carmarthenshire Railway to standard gauge. The principal entrepreneur was John Waddell of Edinburgh, a member of a well-known family of contractors, which helped to finance, build and manage the railway. The L&MMR opened for traffic on 1st January 1883 and, after the opening of collieries belonging to the Waddell family in 1887, its length was extended to no less than 13 miles. In this distance the line climbed to an altitude of 500 feet above sea level, the ruling gradient for several miles being 1 in 40, and there were tight curves which also slowed down operations. The GWR took over in 1922 and even at that time it was not unusual to see the remarkable spectacle of three locomotives on a train – two at the front and a banker pushing mightily at the rear. The L&MMR had an office in Llanelly and while they did not operate a public passenger service they are said to have carried 130,000 colliers annually in a fleet of eight workmen's carriages and sometimes ran passenger trips at holiday times. In the early 1920s the line is reputed to have transported 420,000 tons of coal per year to the docks at Llanelly. In this picture 1600 Class 0-6-0PT No.1643, of Llanelly shed, is seen shunting at Cynheidre colliery on 3rd September 1965 during the course of working a coal train to Burry Port. Within a few weeks of this scene being recorded No.1643 was withdrawn from service, Llanelly shed was closed in November, and very shortly afterwards steam traction was banished from South Wales. *Roy Denison*

THE LLANELLY TO CROSS HANDS MINERAL LINE

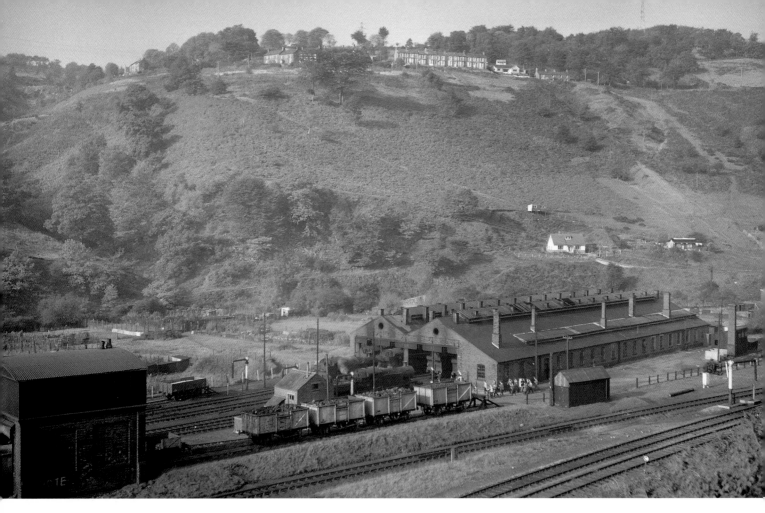

The very dense network of lines, and extremely heavy coal and general goods traffic in South Wales, ensured that an engine shed was located at almost every railway centre of any importance. This was the shed at Aberbeeg, photographed from a high vantage point, on 14th October 1962. This four-road building was opened on 7th April 1919, replacing a much smaller Monmouthshire Railway & Canal Company shed that for more than sixty years had stood a few hundred yards to the north. It is recorded that on a Sunday morning the shed was usually full of silent locomotives, which were often outnumbered by a herd of extremely noisy sheep. Aberbeeg shed was closed at the end of December 1964, sold for commercial use and converted into an iron foundry.
W. Potter / R.C. Riley collection

Almost unbelieveably, a total of seven sheds was built at Aberdare over the years to house locomotives primarily engaged on moving coal trains from the Dare and Cynon valleys. The Aberdare Railway constructed two short-lived sheds, followed in 1864 by the Vale of Neath Railway's shed. The Taff Vale Railway's depot opened during the following year but it was closed in 1927. The GWR built a four-road shed in 1867 and seven years later it was doubled in size as a result of booming traffic. The seventh, and last shed to be constructed at Aberdare, is depicted here with the repair shop prominent on the extreme left; this single turntable shed opened on 11th November 1907 and replaced the eight-road shed. This photograph was taken on 14th October 1962 and shows 5600 Class 0-6-2Ts Nos. 6622 and 5625 standing at the coaling stage. At the beginning of 1965 the shed had an allocation of 12 engines but closed on 1st March.
W. Potter / R.C. Riley collection

An industrial haze? In this shot, taken at Pontypool Road on the same day as the previous two pictures, smoke from locomotives' chimneys drifts across the shed's hinterland, almost obscuring the hill beyond. In steam days engine sheds were often blanketed by (what sometimes seemed to be) a permanent pall of smoke and Pontypool Road was clearly no exception. The establishment here, the GWR's second turntable shed, opened in 1865 and was almost immediately extended by the addition of an eight-road straight shed. The latter originally had wooden doors and a wood-and-tile roof, but this was replaced by corrugated asbestos at some stage. In 1898 the GWR constructed a substantial coaling stage with a pitched roof: this had three tips and there was a sand house adjacent. The shed lasted 100 years, closing in May 1965, and by this time its allocation had shrunk to just a handful of tank locomotives. *W. Potter / R.C.Riley collection*

Around a fifth of the 251 Class 9F 2-10-0s were allocated to the WR in the early 1960s and even in 1964, when rapid dieselisation was making substantial inroads into the steam classes, about 30 of these machines were still based on the Region, predominantly in South Wales. The vast bulk of these extremely competent locomotives was built at Crewe but No.92206, seen here near Undy, west of Severn Tunnel Junction, was one of 43 members of the 9F class constructed at Swindon works from where this particular example emerged in May 1959. Regrettably, like many of its sister engines, No.92206 was destined to have a pathetically short working life being withdrawn in May 1967. The 9F was working an empty iron ore train on 14th May 1965. Note the water troughs laid between the rails of both the up and down fast tracks and the water tank feeding them on the left. Troughs were laid by three of the pre-nationalisation companies, the only exception being the Southern Railway. They were an important part of everyday railway operation, enabling locomotives to refill their tenders at speed; there were three sets of troughs between London and Cardiff. *Hugh Ballantyne*

Friday 8th September 1961 was a sad day for WR steam fans, particularly in South Wales, because it saw the last, regular steam-hauled runs of the 'South Wales Pullman', eight-car Blue Pullman diesel-electric units taking over from the following Monday. Prior to the introduction of the winter timetable on 11th September the down working left London at 8.50am while the up train from Swansea departed at 4.30pm. This service pattern was completely altered with the morning train leaving Swansea at 6.40am while the scheduled departure of the evening train from Paddington was at 4.55pm. Passengers on the up train benefited from an acceleration which introduced a 3hr 35min journey time from Swansea to London – the fastest ever. The down train was, however, kept on a slower schedule similar to the fastest steam-worked train on the route. This was not quite the total eclipse of steam on the 'South Wales Pullman', however, because the set of Pullman cars formerly used was kept in reserve for use when the diesel unit was unavailable. In this picture the final morning down train from Paddington is seen at Cardiff (General) on 8th September with immaculate 'Castle' Class 4-6-0 No.5048 *Earl of Devon* in charge. *Hugh Ballantyne*

Swansea (High Street) is the location of this portrait of 'Castle' Class 4-6-0 No.4090 *Dorchester Castle* awaiting departure with the last regular up steam-hauled 'South Wales Pullman' on the afternoon of 8th September 1961. Needless to say the locomotive had been turned out in absolutely sparkling condition by Landore shed. It is interesting to note that at the time the first class Pullman supplement from Swansea to Paddington was a trifling ten shillings (50p), whilst the ordinary first class single fare between those points was £3. Those were the days! It is worth noting that those prices were equal to about £9 and £54 at the time of writing. *Hugh Ballantyne*

Carmarthen has a colourful railway history by virtue of the fact that no fewer than eight different companies served the town in the nineteenth century. These included the optimistically named Carmarthen & Cardigan Railway, which never reached Cardigan, and the ridiculously ambitious Manchester & Milford Railway which built only a short stretch of line north of Carmarthen, and got nowhere near Manchester nor Milford Haven. Most of the small concerns were absorbed into the GWR, one notable exception being the mighty LNWR(!) which operated from Llandilo along a line acquired by that company in 1871, thus giving it a foothold in the Welsh town. The South Wales Railway (SWR) reached Carmarthen in the early 1850s, the first trains running on 11th October 1852. The ultimate objective of the SWR was Fishguard, however, and due to Carmarthen town's position on a hilltop it was decided to take the main line along a direct course to the west, south of the town, and construct Carmarthen's station at the north end of a triangle on the east bank of the river Towy. Thus, through passenger trains from Swansea to Fishguard and vice versa via Carmarthen would have to reverse, but other workings not required to stop there could avoid the station completely. In this portrait, taken on 25th May 1963, 'Hall' Class 4-6-0 No.4962 *Ragley Hall* is seen awaiting departure from Carmarthen at 2.50pm with the 'Pembroke Coast Express' for Paddington. In the 1961 summer timetable this train was advertised to leave Pembroke Dock at 1.05pm and the booked arrival time in London was 7.50pm; on Saturdays the train made additional stops and arrived in Paddington at 8.25pm. *Edwin Wilmshurst*

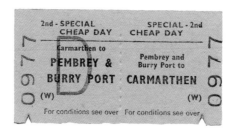

Whitland station, 13¼ miles from Carmarthen, is the junction for the branch to Tenby and Pembroke Dock, and the former line to Cardigan which lost its passenger service way back in 1962 before 'Beeching' became a household name. Strangely, for a time Whitland was served by both broad and standard gauge trains, this being a result of 'railway politics' in the area. The SWR broad gauge, double track line from Carmarthen had reached Whitland by about 1851, while the Pembroke & Tenby Railway's standard gauge line opened to Whitland on 4th September 1866, and this ambitious company threatened to build its own route through to Carmarthen where it could connect with the LNWR. In order to put a stop to this impudence the GWR converted one of its tracks between Whitland and Carmarthen to standard gauge and so two gauges operated until the general gauge conversion in South Wales was carried out in 1872. The station was remodelled in the late 1950s and had a down island platform with an arrival bay on the up side; a small locomotive depot, a sub-shed of Neyland, housed engines that worked the branches. Perhaps the most important feature of Whitland was the large milk depot east of the station which provided a huge amount of traffic for the railway. Whitland station's modern design can be seen in this picture of 'Hall' Class 4-6-0 No.6984 *Owsden Hall* awaiting departure with the 12.04pm Milford Haven to Swansea train on 25th May 1963. *Edwin Wilmshurst*

A locomotive shed was constructed by the GWR at Goodwick when the Fishguard route was opened to traffic in 1906. The shed was an unpretentious two-road affair and the GWR wisely built a small depot which was laid out in such a way to permit easy expansion if necessary – note the open tracks to the left of the shed. There was a corrugated coaling stage and 12,000 gallon water tank. In the event the anticipated increase in traffic was never attained and the shed remained more or less as built until closure occurred in September 1963. Part of the village of Goodwick, on the hill above the shed, provides the backdrop. Interestingly, the name Fishguard Harbour was not really accurate, the nearest place to the harbour being Goodwick, but when it came to the name of the locomotive depot it was known as Goodwick shed, reflecting the fact that it was situated in the village of that name. *Edwin Wilmshurst*

Extract from Western Region winter 1953–54 timetable

In bygone days the junction signal at Clarbeston Road, where the Fishguard Harbour and Milford Haven lines diverge, had the signal for the former on the lower doll post indicating that the Fishguard line was regarded as the branch. The Milford Haven line dated from 1863 but the Fishguard route was a much later arrival on the scene, not opening throughout until 1906. In the early 1960s Fishguard had a very modest train service consisting of a few fast boat trains to and from Paddington, supplemented by a meagre local service to Clarbeston Road which connected with 'main line' services from Neyland and Milford Haven. In this photograph, taken on 25th May 1963, 8750 Class 0-6-0PT No.9602 is seen running in to Fishguard and Goodwick station with a local working from Clarbeston Road. The building behind the station nameboard is the locomotive shed's coaling plant, the main shed building being out of sight, hidden by the train. *Edwin Wilmshurst*

The first section of the 56 miles-long Carmarthen to Aberystwyth line was opened from Carmarthen to Conwil on 3rd September 1860 by the Carmarthen & Cardigan Railway (C&CR) which had obtained its Act of Parliament on 7th August 1854. The C&CR, however, could not meet hire charges for rolling stock and the service was suspended at the end of December but resumed from 12th August 1861. The second stretch of line – from Conwil to Pencader – was apparently opened for passenger traffic on 28th March 1864 before approval had been given by the Board of Trade which was very unhappy about Pencader station being built on a 1 in 60 incline. In November 1864, however, all work came to an abrupt halt when the C&CR was put into the hands of a receiver with debts of more than £1m. The next section of the route, from Pencader to Lampeter (12¼ miles), was built by the Manchester & Milford Railway (M&MR), a company with wild and totally unrealistic ambitions to link the northern city with Milford Haven. This section of line was opened on New Year's Day 1866 without being sanctioned by the Board of Trade – history had repeated itself.

Lampeter to Strata Florida followed on 1st September 1866; this section was also built by the M&MR. The line turned sharply westwards after Strata Florida, climbing out of the vale of Teifi on a 1 in 41 gradient to emerge high above the wooded Ystwyth valley. This final stretch of M&MR line on to Aberystwyth (14½ miles) was brought into use on 12th August 1867. The service along this stretch of line, which had been the last to be opened, proved to be the first to close when the rail passenger service was withdrawn following flooding in December 1964, buses being provided until the official closure date. Passenger services along the entire route ceased from 22nd February 1965 when Wales lost one of its least known and most remote rural lines but it should be noted that sections of the route remained open for goods traffic for some years afterwards. Immediately after departure from Carmarthen station, trains on the Aberystwyth line crossed the Afon Tywi on this fine girder bridge which is nicely reflected in the still waters. An unknown 2251 Class 0-6-0, hauling a modest two-coach train, heads northwards on 18th May 1961 with the distant hills giving just a hint of the delightful journey that lies ahead. *John Spencer Gilks*

Between Bronwydd Arms and Conwil the line follows the very steeply sided and thickly wooded valley of the Afon Gwili, twisting and turning with the course of the river and on some occasions actually forced to run in a south-westerly direction. In this photograph an Aberystwyth to Carmarthen train is seen leaving Conwil station on 30th June 1962 behind a rather dirty 'Manor' Class 4-6-0 No.7804 *Baydon Manor* from Llanelly shed. Despite the very narrow defile at this point the railway authorities have just managed to squeeze in a water tank and signal and even found room for Conwil station a few yards further back. *John Spencer Gilks*

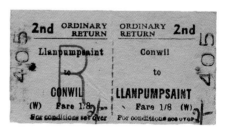

A portrait of Llangybi station taken on the same day as the previous shot. The luxuriant, unrestricted growth of weeds suggests that the 'presentation' of this station was very low on BR's priorities. Receipts from passengers joining trains at Llangybi were probably miniscule as a result of the village being situated on the Lampeter to Tregaron main road and a bus service no doubt provided a more frequent and convenient service for local people. This station was a request stop and passengers wishing to alight had to inform the guard at the previous station, while those wishing to join had to give a hand signal to the driver during daylight only. *Rodney Lissenden*

A Carmarthen to Aberystwyth train, headed by BR Standard Class 4MT 4-6-0 No.75029, enters the tiny and no doubt little-used station at Llangybi, between Lampeter and Tregaron, on 18th July 1962. Amazing though it may seem the photographer was not moving around the area by car but was actually a *bona fide* passenger travelling to Aberystwyth. He was on a week-long holiday with two friends and they had previously journeyed overnight from London to Carmarthen and used this line to reach their isolated holiday cottage which was located 'in the middle of nowhere' about a three miles-long walk from the station. The considerable amount of walking involved, coupled with the fact that the only water available at the cottage had to be pumped up from the bowels of the earth, perhaps gives the impression that this was more of a week-long endurance test but it was no doubt great fun. One wonders how many photographs of Llangybi station exist, especially ones taken by a genuine passenger! There was another station of the same name on the Afon Wen to Caernarvon line so, presumably, one could have purchased a ticket from one Llangybi to another! *Rodney Lissenden*

Built primarily to serve the small hamlet of Ty'n-y-graig, as well as providing access to a local attraction, Caradog Falls Halt was opened by the GWR on 5th September 1932. The platform appears to be of the cheap 'wood and ash' type which was commonly used by the GWR at that time – after all there was no point in spending heavily on a new station that might not produce the anticipated returns. The halt was in a very peaceful setting surrounded by fields and woodland and just a few cottages, the main Tregaron to Aberystwyth road being behind the photographer on a higher level. This picture of the halt shows an unknown 4300 Class 'Mogul' leaving with a train *en route* to Carmarthen. Unlike other halts on the line which were request stops, it was mandatory for most trains to stop at Caradog Falls. *John Spencer Gilks*

Extract from Western Region winter 1953–54 timetable

| Table 146 | | CARMARTHEN, PENCADER, and ABERYSTWYTH | | | |

(Timetable image – detailed departure and arrival times)

A smoky departure. Some of the toughest climbing on the WR could be found on the Carmarthen to Aberystwyth line with gradients as steep as 1 in 41, and many very tight curves to make life even more difficult for enginemen. Generally, 2½ hours were allowed for the 56¼ miles which separated the towns, the generous timings no doubt reflecting the arduous nature of the route and also the fact that there were 21 intermediate stations, though not all were mandatory stops. The hard work started for the crew almost immediately after leaving Aberystwyth because trains on the Carmarthen line curved away very sharply on a 1 in 42 gradient up to a bridge which took them across the Afon Rheidol. The narrow gauge Vale of Rheidol line, which ran underneath the first span of the bridge, is hidden from view behind the stone wall. So, the crew will have already got an idea of the job that lies ahead but at least a powerful engine such as BR Standard Class 4MT 2-6-4T No.80096 should make their task easier. This photograph was taken during the summer of 1963. *Derek Penney*

CARMARTHEN TO ABERYSTWYTH

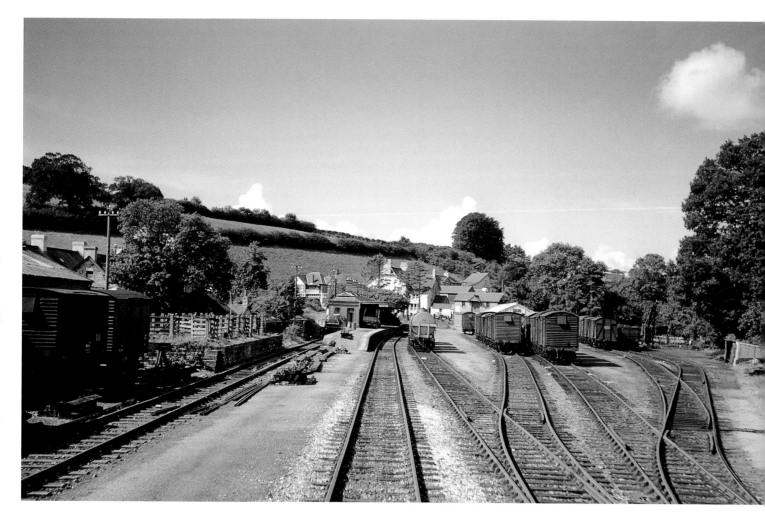

During the railway mania in 1845/46 many crackpot, ridiculously optimistic schemes were put forward, and among them were the plans of the Carmarthen & Cardigan Railway (C&CR) who proposed not only a broad gauge link between the two towns via Newcastle Emlyn, but also 23 miles of associated mineral lines running south-eastwards to Cross Hands and Kidwelly to connect with other lines. The prime object, however, was to link London with 'the important seaport and town of Cardigan' and it was envisaged that Cardigan would oust Holyhead as the main port for Ireland – wishful thinking indeed. The C&CR obtained an Act on 7th August 1854 to build the first section to Newcastle Emlyn and construction commenced in 1857, but by late 1858 its finances were in a bad way with the company secretary being accused by shareholders of acting in a high-handed manner. Despite these problems the six miles-long section to Conwil opened on 3rd September 1860 and the line had reached Llandyssul (17½ miles from Carmarthen) by June 1864. Five months later, however, the C&CR, with debts of over £1m, found itself in the hands of the receiver, its grandiose plans in tatters and all hope of reaching Cardigan gone. Eventually, the seven miles-long stretch from Llandyssul to Newcastle Emlyn was completed by the GWR, this opening on 1st July 1895. Passenger services were withdrawn from the Newcastle Emlyn branch as long ago as 15th September 1952, but goods traffic was buoyant and lasted until 1973. In this picture, taken on a bright and sunny 18th August 1962, the goods yard at Newcastle Emlyn certainly seems to be busy. *John Langford*

G. W. R.

Newcastle Emlyn

A lost way of life. In bygone times crossing keepers were responsible, as the title suggests, for ensuring the level crossing of which they had charge was open to rail-borne traffic. Usually, the keepers were in constant communication with adjacent signal boxes regarding train movements but on lightly used, goods-only routes where train speeds were low they sometimes relied on the train crews to sound the engine's whistle at the appropriate time. This charming scene was recorded at Glantwelly crossing on 18th August 1962 from the brake van of the 11.25am goods from Newcastle Emlyn to Carmarthen Junction. The crossing keeper (or possibly the train's guard on this occasion) is closing the gates watched by a lady and little girl on the left of the photograph. Passage of the daily goods was probably the highlight of the day and they could resume their relaxed routine once it had passed through. *John Langford*

Henllan station looks extraordinarily neat and tidy, apart from the grassy platform surfaces, in this illustration and it is difficult to believe that it had been closed for almost ten years when this shot was taken in August 1962. The locomotive in view is 8750 Class pannier tank engine No.9606, working the 11.25am goods from Newcastle Emlyn, and this shot was taken on the same day as the previous two pictures. The signal box, with its patterned brickwork, is a delight and perhaps the open door can be explained by the fact that the guard has 'opened up' to permit some shunting to take place. The goods shed can just be discerned on the extreme left. *John Langford*

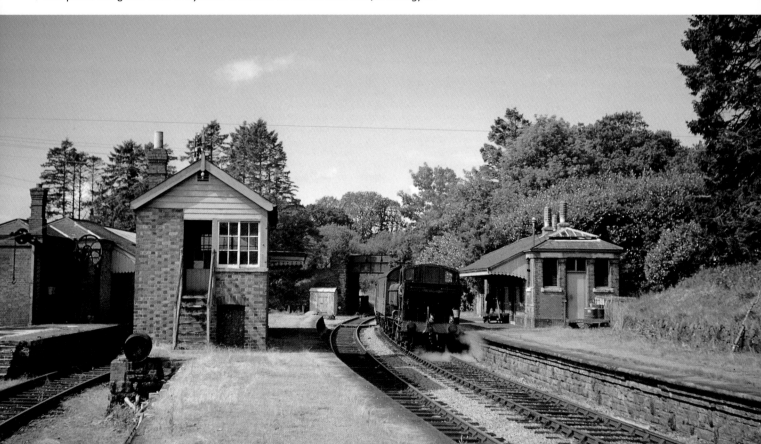

The 11.25am Newcastle Emlyn to Carmarthen Junction branch goods working is seen again, with nicely cleaned 8750 Class 0-6-0PT No.9606 in charge, and is depicted waiting for the 'road' at Pencader Junction on 18th August 1962. *John Langford*

The first stage of the branch from Whitland to Cardigan was incorporated on 12th July 1869; this was the Whitland & Taf Vale Railway (W&TVR) which was proposed with the objective of serving the important slate quarries at Glogue, fourteen miles from Whitland. It should be noted that this river Taf rises above Glogue and should not be confused with the more widely known river Taff in Glamorganshire. The W&TVR was actually authorised to build a branch as far as Crymmych Arms, 16½ miles from Whitland, and the first stretch of line was opened as far as Llanfyrnach (12¾ miles from Whitland) on 24th March 1873, the remaining 3¾ miles on to Crymmych Arms opening during October of the following year. In 1877 the W&TVR obtained powers to continue to Cardigan and consequently changed its name to 'Whitland & Cardigan' which was much more appropriate. When this final section was opened on 1st September 1886 the GWR took over the operation of the line which was merely a precursor to the GWR absorbing the local company four years later. Perhaps it should be mentioned that of all the branch lines featured in this album the Cardigan branch had a very poor, slow and seemingly inconvenient service of four up and three down trains on weekdays only. For reasons not known to the author in the 1954/55 winter timetable there were two morning passenger workings from Cardigan at 6.55am and 9.50am and then a very long gap during the day until the final train to Whitland departed at 5.45pm, so it was hard luck for any passengers who missed the 9.50am – perhaps there was a competing bus service upon which they could fall back. It probably came as no shock to the local populace when the passenger service, such as existed, was withdrawn on 10th September 1962 and the goods trains did not last much longer. The branch was extremely picturesque but the almost deserted station and countryside at Login exemplify the reasons for its unprofitability; a 4500 Class 2-6-2T, No.4557, hauling the 4.00pm train from Whitland to Cardigan, pauses there on 31st May 1962. *John Spencer Gilks*

Table 150	WHITLAND, CRYMMYCH ARMS, and CARDIGAN									
Miles		Week Days only				Miles		Week Days only		
		a.m	a.m	p.m	p.m			a.m	a.m	p.m
	Whitland..........dep	6 30	1130	4 0	6 15		Cardigan..........dep	7 0	9 50	5 45 ..
3½	Llanfalteg..........	6 40	1140	4 10	6 25	3	Kilgerran..........	7 9	9 59	5 54 ..
6	Login..........	6 50	1150	4 20	6 36	6½	Boncath..........	7 24	1014	6 9 ..
8½	Llanglydwen..........	7 3	12 2	4 32	6 57	11	Crymmych Arms......	7 37	1027	6 22 ..
10½	Rhydowen..........	7 9	12 8	4 38	7 3	13½	Glogue..........	7 48	1038	6 33 ..
12½	Llanfyrnach..........	7 18	1217	4 46	7 12	14½	Llanfyrnach..........	7 55	1044	6 40 ..
14	Glogue..........	7 27	1225	4 54	7 20	17½	Rhydowen..........	8 4	1053	6 49 ..
16½	Crymmych Arms ;.....	7 39	1235	5 4	7 30	18½	Llanglydwen..........	8 10	11 0	6 56 ..
21	Boncath..........	7 52	1248	5 17	7 43	21½	Login..........	8 22	1110	7 7 ..
24½	Kilgerran..........	8 2	1258	5 27	7 53	23½	Llanfalteg..........	8 33	1120	7 17 ..
27½	Cardigan D......arr	8 11	1 7	5 36	8 2	27½	Whitland..........arr	8 43	1131	7 29 ..

D Station for Gwbert-on-Sea (3½ miles)

Extract from Western Region winter 1953–54 timetable

Photographed not long after sunrise on 18th August 1962, the 6.20am Whitland to Cardigan train headed by rather dirty 4500 Class 2-6-2T No.4569 waits at Llanfyrnach as two railwaymen and the local postman observe the antics of the photographer, no doubt with some amusement. At least they were guaranteed one passenger! Interestingly, the 6.20am was officially classified as a 'mixed' train which meant it was booked to convey passengers, and goods traffic as required. The photographer comments, however, that on this particular day, which was a Saturday, it was running as a passenger train, there being no goods vehicles attached. The Cardigan branch generally followed the sinuous course of the Afon Taf and at Llanfyrnach the river is running in a more or less north easterly direction, and when it abruptly changes to run in a north westerly direction the railway did likewise. *John Langford*

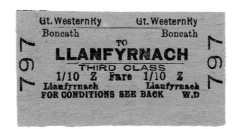

Dedication rewarded! Photographers had to get up very early indeed if they wanted to photograph the 6.20am Whitland to Cardigan train and it is likely that in this case the photographer had journeyed down to Whitland overnight from London which, in those far off days, was quite a civilised way of travelling if there was an available compartment where one could 'stretch out'. In this case the contributor was blessed with brilliant early morning sunshine when the 6.20am *ex*-Whitland, with 4500 Class 2-6-2T No.4569 in charge, paused at Boncath on 18th August 1962. No doubt this picture was taken with the co-operation of the engine crew because if they had departed before the photographer had clambered back on board he would have had a five hour wait until the next train to Cardigan was due. Boncath was only 21 miles from Whitland but, amazingly, this train was booked to take more than 1½ hours to cover this distance so it was obviously not intended for passengers in a hurry. *John Langford*

G. W. R.

BONCATH

A GWR-designed pannier tank locomotive on the Cardigan branch. 1600 Class 0-6-0PT No.1666 simmers in Cardigan station on 22nd August 1962 after arrival with the 11.35am from Whitland which is formed of two coaches rather than the usual one normally provided for trains on the branch. Note the public notice on the side of the station building which doubtless stated that withdrawal of the passenger service had been approved by the Ministry of Transport and listed substitute bus services that would be run to alleviate any hardship caused by the cessation of the train service. No.1666 was one of a class of 70 locomotives designed by Hawksworth for the GWR but in fact all of the locomotives were built during the BR era with the last, including No.1666, entering service in the mid-1950s so many had very short working lives. The wagons visible in the goods yard, and parcels being unloaded from the guard's brake van, create an illusion that the line was doing good business – sadly the last passenger working left Cardigan less than three weeks after this shot was taken. *R.C.Riley collection*

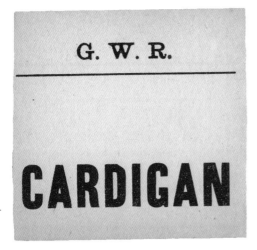

A view of the approach to Neyland station, taken on 25th May 1963, with 8750 Class 0-6-0PT No. 4654 pottering around in the foreground. The locomotive shed, on the extreme left of the picture, was opened as a broad gauge shed in 1856 by the South Wales Railway and apparently comprised the re-erected, former engine shed from Chepstow (West) which only lasted from 1850 to 1855 at its original location. Later, at an unknown date, a further building was added to accommodate Neyland's increasing allocation. The shed was exceptional because it had an entrance for one road at the northern end and a two-road entrance at the other end and, doubtless, this was a legacy of its piecemeal evolution. Presumably the one-road section was the older of the two which was formerly used at Chepstow. There was a 65 foot-long turntable and lofty pumphouse that towered above the shed environs. The residents of the cottages on the hill overlooking the shed probably took a dim view of BR's activities only a few yards away – one wonders if they ever obtained a reduction in their rates because of the endless noise and smoke. Perhaps if they worked on the railway their objections would have been much more muted. *Edwin Wilmshurst*

The single track, broad gauge branch from Haverfordwest to Neyland (the SWR's principal port for Ireland) was opened on 15th April 1856. Neyland was, perhaps, a curious choice for the SWR's main embarkation port to Ireland, bearing in mind the close proximity of both Milford Haven and Pembroke Dock. Even worse, the distance to Waterford was nearly 40 sea miles longer than it would have been from Fishguard to Rosslare. Perhaps

the SWR itself had qualms about the decision to opt for Neyland because it seemed to be in turmoil over what to call it, the name 'New Milford' being used for a time until Neyland was settled upon in 1906. It was in that year that the GWR re-routed the Irish traffic to Fishguard Harbour but Neyland retained much of its importance due to its fish and coal traffic, and it was also a focal point of local railway operations because the locomotive depot that supplied much of the power for main line and local services was located there. The Neyland branch later withered, however, public goods traffic ceasing from 2nd December 1963 while the last passenger trains ran on 14th June 1964. Some of the somewhat basic buildings are seen in this view of Neyland station and this scene was recorded on 21st August 1961 when through trains to and from Paddington – including overnight services – were still in operation. Extra caution was required by the drivers of trains coming into the station: if they overshot the platform and demolished the buffer stops they could finish up in the deep waters of the haven. *Edwin Wilmshurst*

Various schemes for a railway serving Devil's Bridge were proposed, and if the Manchester & Milford Railway's (M&MR) idea, dating from 1861, of a standard gauge line across the mountains from near Llanidloes to Alltddu (north of Tregaron) had come to fruition, Devil's Bridge would have been the site of a junction station where passengers were able to change for Aberystwyth! In the event, almost inevitably, this scheme fell by the wayside and the present Vale of Rheidol line (VoR) was promoted by a company of that name who obtained an Act on 6th August 1897. Built to bring lead ore and timber down to Aberystwyth, the line opened for goods traffic in August 1902 and on 22nd December for passengers, following the route of the M&MR's 1861 proposal. There was a ½ mile-long branch to Aberystwyth harbour, but the principal feature is undoubtedly the dramatic and highly scenic ascent to Devil's Bridge, the climb commencing five miles from Aberystwyth with a ruling gradient of 1 in 48; the line rises 670 feet over its total length. In August 1913 the line was sold to the Cambrian Railways, but shortly afterwards the First World War intervened and all traffic declined; the GWR acquired it in 1922. Daily passenger trains ceased in January 1931, the VoR becoming a summer-only attraction, and the line was mothballed during the Second World War, re-opening in July 1945. Remarkably, the VoR has had three separate terminal stations in Aberystwyth over the years, the first being merely a spur off the harbour branch and somewhat inconvenient for prospective passengers arriving at the main station. The harbour branch was closed in 1924 (the rails being lifted in 1930) and the opportunity was taken to extend the tracks across the former Smithfield Road to a new terminus beside the standard gauge station, the new station opening in 1925. In 1968 the VoR line, which had previously followed the sinuous course of the Afon Rheidol for the last half a mile into Aberystwyth, was completely realigned to run alongside the main line into the main station, where VoR trains used the former Carmarthen line platform which was available following the withdrawal of trains on that route in 1965. In this picture, taken in the summer of 1955, No.8 *Llywelyn* is seen easing across Smithfield Road with (what appears to be) a train of empty coaching stock. A BR flagman is in attendance while a local lad with time on his hands surveys the scene from the top of a fence. While the superb VoR line is still very much in business this interesting section of the route in the 'suburbs' of Aberystwyth has disappeared. BR tried their best to make the locomotives look ridiculous by painting them in corporate blue livery, a huge indignity for 'Swindon' products, while later the three locomotives achieved fame as the very last steam engines in the BR fleet. *Colin Hogg*

G.W.R.
Aberystwyth

A Welsh hill station. The magnificent surroundings of Devil's Bridge station are exemplified in this shot which was taken on 26th August 1959 – the landscape would have looked even more appealing if the sun had been shining! Remarkably, if the Manchester & Milford Railway's fanciful proposal for a standard gauge Llanidloes to Tregaron route had come to fruition there could have been a junction station on this site or thereabouts! *Roy Denison*

The history of the Welshpool & Llanfair Light Railway can be traced back as far as 1818 because part of the route in Welshpool was built on an ancient tramway. Various ideas were aired for a line west of Welshpool and a standard gauge line actually got as far as receiving the Royal Assent in 1877 but, like earlier schemes, it was later abandoned. There was even disagreement between local people regarding the gauge of the line but in the event the Welshpool & Llanfair Company obtained a light railway order on 8th September 1899 for a 2ft 6in gauge line just over 9 miles long. The Cambrian Railways (CR) agreed to construct and maintain the line which started in the CR's yard at Welshpool main line station and crossed the Montgomeryshire canal before threading its way through the town, crossing streets before disappearing between houses. The principal landmarks on the route are the 1 in 30 Golfa bank and a three-span steel girder bridge across the river Banwy, near Heniarth. The W&LLR opened for goods traffic on 9th March 1903 and for regular passengers two days later. The line remained independent until taken over by the GWR in 1923 but that railway's bus service from Welshpool to Dinas Mawddwy, introduced in 1925, creamed off the W&LLR's passenger traffic to such an extent that passenger trains were withdrawn from 9th February 1931. The line closed completely in 1956, the final train under BR auspices being an enthusiasts' special on 3rd November. The line partially re-opened as a tourist attraction in 1963 but the fascinating section through the town at Welshpool had to be sacrificed for the inevitable road improvements. In this charming picture 0-6-0T No.822 *The Earl,* a Beyer Peacock product of 1902, attracts the attention of a little girl walking along with her mother as it weaves between houses and parked cars in Welshpool town centre during the summer of 1956 shortly before closure. In the background the clock tower of St Mary's church indicates that the time was 2.25pm, but the record of the precise date has been lost. *Colin Hogg*

G. W. R.

WELSHPOOL

Llanfair station (or Llanfair P.G. as it is sometimes known) is probably one of the most famous stations in Great Britain on account of its full name which consists of 58 letters, the lengthy station nameboard being prominent in this shot of 'Royal Scot' Class 7P 4-6-0 No.46150 *The Life Guardsman* which is seen drawing to a halt with a down local train, probably the 1.00pm Llandudno Junction to Holyhead, on 24th May 1962. Llanfair, the first station on Anglesey from the Chester direction, was opened on 1st August 1848 when a purely local service operated to and from Holyhead prior to the commissioning of the Britannia bridge across the Menai Strait. When this picture was taken the station appears to be in a tidy condition with attractive flower beds. Llanfair was closed to passengers from 14th February 1966 but reopened as a temporary exchange platform on 29th May 1970 following the fire that closed the Britannia bridge; it was closed again on 31st January 1972 when services across the bridge were restored. But that was not the end of Llanfair station because it was permanently reopened on 7th May 1973 and is still very much in business at the time of writing. *John Spencer Gilks*

TAILPIECE